Moravian Church in America

## Offices of Worship and Hymns

Principally for use in schools - with an appendix of tunes. Second Edition

Moravian Church in America

**Offices of Worship and Hymns**
*Principally for use in schools - with an appendix of tunes. Second Edition*

ISBN/EAN: 9783337286125

Printed in Europe, USA, Canada, Australia, Japan

Cover: Foto ©Lupo / pixelio.de

More available books at **www.hansebooks.com**

# OFFICES OF WORSHIP

AND

# HYMNS,

PRINCIPALLY FOR USE IN SCHOOLS.

WITH AN APPENDIX OF TUNES.

SECOND AND REVISED EDITION.

BETHLEHEM, PA.:
MORAVIAN PUBLICATION OFFICE.
1883.

# PREFACE
## TO THE SECOND EDITION.

With the exceptions stated below, the hymns in the first edition have been retained in this. Many desirable changes suggested themselves, both as regards the arrangement and omission of hymns, and the introduction of new ones, but it was on the whole deemed best to make as few of these as possible, inasmuch as a large number of copies of the first edition is still in use. Besides verbal or other slight corrections in the text of the hymns, which have only been adopted after a careful examination of standard authorities, the following are the alterations made in this edition:

In Office of Worship No. IV, the sentence, "May Thy holy birth" etc., with its response, has been omitted, as the idea intended to be conveyed was not always clearly understood.

In the Hymns, Nos. 221 and 281 are new, the one having, in the first edition, been a repetition, and the other was rejected because of its difficult metre.

Four Scriptural litanies have been added to the Offices of Worship. They have been taken, with some modifications, from other collections.

A few new hymns have been added after the Doxologies.

In accordance with various suggestions to that effect, the names of some tunes, and the books in which the Peculiar Metres are found, are given in foot notes. The full titles of these books are given below.

The following statement, which is mainly taken from the Preface to the first edition, presents the principles which guided the compilers in making this selection of hymns.

*First*, principally hymns that are suitable for purposes of worship were chosen. It is a matter of great importance that congregations of children and young persons are made to feel that they are taking part in a service of actual devotion and worship, and therefore the hymns used should help to inspire this feeling. *Secondly*, for the most part, standard hymns have been selected. The hymns which children and youth are to learn and to sing, should be such as are of permanent worth. These once incorporated into the memory, will remain there through life, and be a treasure of Scriptural doctrine, of warning and comfort, which will never be exhausted, and become increasingly valuable with added years and experience. A few hymns, which because of their vivacity and adaptation to youthful feelings, are generally popular, or are suitable for anniversary and other special occasions, have been inserted, though neither their matter nor the influence they are likely to exert entitle them to any other than a very sparing use. *Thirdly*, regard was had to such hymns as are suitable for religious instruction in the family, the catechetical class, and in preparing candidates for confirmation.

The copyright tunes reprinted in the Appendix were used by the special permission of Dr. Lowell Mason and the late Mr. Wm. B. Bradbury.

FEBRUARY, 2, 1872.

The TUNE BOOKS referred to are the following: Plymouth Collection, (A. S. Barnes, New York), S. S. Bell, (Horace Waters, New York), Songs of Devotion, Plymouth S. S. Collection, Golden Chain, Fresh Laurels (Biglow & Main, New York), Happy Voices (American Tract Society), S. S. Hosanna (American S. S. Union), Songs of Gladness (J. C. Garrigues & Co., Philadelphia).

# TABLE OF CONTENTS.

|  | Page |
|---|---|
| OFFICES OF WORSHIP, | 7–31 |
| THE WORD OF GOD, | 33 |
| CREATION AND PROVIDENCE, | 37 |
| Ministry of Angels, | 43 |
| REDEMPTION, | 44 |
| THE COMING OF CHRIST.—Advent, | 47 |
| THE BIRTH OF CHRIST.—Christmas, | 51 |
| THE EPIPHANY, | 61 |
| CHRIST'S LIFE AND EXAMPLE, | 64 |
| Palm Sunday, | 71 |
| THE SUFFERINGS OF CHRIST.—Passion Week, | 72 |
| THE RESURRECTION OF CHRIST.—Easter, | 79 |
| ASCENSION AND GLORY OF CHRIST, | 80 |
| THE HOLY SPIRIT.—Whit Sunday, | 85 |
| THE HOLY TRINITY, | 88 |
| CHRISTIAN LIFE:— | |
| I. INVITATION AND WARNING, | 89 |
| II. REPENTANCE, | 95 |
| III. FAITH, | 102 |
| IV. SELF-CONSECRATION, | 114 |
| V. LOVE, | 119 |

|  |  |
|---|---|
| VI. JOY AND PRAISE, | 133 |
| VII. PRAYER, | 147 |
| VIII. CONFESSION OF CHRIST, | 152 |
| IX. PATIENCE AND TRUST, | 159 |
| THE CHRISTIAN CHURCH AND ITS ORDINANCES, | 169 |
| THE SACRAMENTS:— | 172 |
|   Holy Baptism, | 173 |
|   The Holy Communion, | 173 |
| THE SANCTUARY AND THE LORD'S DAY, | 176 |
| TIME AND ETERNITY, | 181 |
| DEATH, RESURRECTION AND JUDGMENT, | 189 |
| HEAVEN, | 200 |
| LITTLE CHILDREN, | 214 |
| MISSIONARY, | 221 |
| ANNIVERSARY, | 229 |
| PATRIOTIC HYMNS, | 233 |
| ON OPENING A NEW SCHOOL ROOM, | 235 |
| THE YEAR, | 236 |
| MORNING, | 238 |
| EVENING, | 243 |
| BEFORE AND AFTER MEALS, | 246 |
| TEMPERANCE, | 248 |
| TEACHERS' MEETINGS, | 249 |
| OPENING AND CLOSING SCHOOL, | 257 |
| BENEDICTIONS AND DOXOLOGIES, | 262 |
| ADDITIONAL HYMNS, | 266 |
| INDEX, | 271 |
| APPENDIX.—TUNES. | |

# OFFICES OF WORSHIP.

## NO. I.

['The Leader shall say, all standing:]

Remember now thy Creator in the days of thy youth.
Serve Him with gladness, and magnify His Name for ever!

What shall I render unto the Lord for all His benefits towards me? I will take the cup of salvation and call upon the name of the Lord.

If we say that we have no sin we deceive ourselves, and the truth is not in us. If we confess our sins, He is faithful and just to forgive us our sins, and to cleanse us from all unrighteousness.

O Lord, we have sinned against heaven and before Thee, and are no more worthy to be called Thy children. We acknowledge our transgressions unto Thee. Have mercy upon us, O Lord; according to Thy loving kindness, and the multitude of Thy tender mercies, blot out our transgressions, through Jesus Christ, our Saviour. Amen.

Lord God, our Father, who art in heaven,

Hallowed be Thy name; Thy kingdom come; Thy will be done in earth as it is in heaven; give us this day our daily bread; and forgive us our trespasses, as we forgive them that trespass against us; and lead us not into temptation, but deliver us from evil; for Thine is the kingdom, and the power, and the glory, for ever and ever: Amen.

Lord God, Son, Thou Saviour of the world,

Be gracious unto us.

By all the merits of Thy life, sufferings, death and resurrection;
*Bless us, gracious Lord and God.*

May Thy blessed humanity on earth,
*Teach us to prize our human nature.*

May Thy holy childhood,
Thy obedience and diligence,
Thy subjection to Thy parents' will,
*Be our comfort and example.*

From indifference to Thy merits and death,
From levity and self-will,
From hypocrisy and deceit,
From the wiles of Satan,
From all neglect of Thy holy will,
From a worldly and selfish mind,
From every form of sin,
*Preserve us, gracious Lord and God.*

Lord God, Holy Ghost,
*Abide with us forever.*

[Then shall all unite in singing the following or some other suitable hymn.]

T. 22.

Since Thou, O holy Lamb of God,
Didst take on Thee our flesh and blood,
Since Thou for us hast lived and died,
Our human nature's sanctified.
Thy youth, unspotted, full of grace,
Teach us all virtue to embrace.
Be Thou our pattern; grant that we
In all things may resemble Thee!

[Then may follow a Scripture lesson, and a short address and prayer, after which shall be said the Apostles' Creed, all standing and repeating together.]

*I believe in God, the Father Almighty, Maker of heaven and earth.*

## OFFICES OF WORSHIP. NO. 1.

*And in Jesus Christ His only Son, our Lord; who was conceived by the Holy Ghost, born of the Virgin Mary, suffered under Pontius Pilate, was crucified, dead and buried; He descended into hell\*; the third day He rose from the dead; He ascended into heaven, and sitteth on the right hand of God the Father Almighty; from thence He shall come to judge the quick and the dead.*

*I believe in the Holy Ghost; the holy catholic† church; the communion of saints; the forgiveness of sins; the resurrection of the body, and the life everlasting.*

*Amen.*

Unto the Lamb that was slain,
  *And hath redeemed us out of all nations of the earth;*
Unto the Lord who purchased our souls for Himself;
  *Unto that Friend who loved us,—and washed us from our sins in His own blood;*
Who died for us once,
  *That we might die unto sin;*
Who rose for us,
  *That we also might rise;*
Who ascended for us into heaven,
  *To prepare a place for us;*
And to whom are subjected the angels, and powers, and dominions,
  To Him be glory at all times,
*In the Church that waiteth for Him, and in that which is around Him.*
From everlasting to everlasting:
*Amen.*

[Then shall all unite in singing:]

The grace of our Lord Jesus Christ,
And the love of God,
And the communion of the Holy Ghost,
Be with us all.  Amen.

---

\* i. e., the grave, or the place of departed spirits.
† i. e., universal.

## NO. II.

[The Leader shall say, all standing:]

Blessed is the man that walketh not in the counsel of the ungodly, nor standeth in the way of sinners, nor sitteth in the seat of the scornful.
*But his delight is in the law of the Lord; and in his law doth he meditate day and night.*

O Lord, Thou hast searched me and known me.
*Thou knowest my down-sitting and mine up-rising, Thou understandest my thoughts afar off.*

Thou compassest my path and my lying down, and art acquainted with all my ways.
*For there is not a word in my tongue, but lo, O Lord, Thou knowest it altogether.*

Search me, O God, and know my heart; try me and know my thoughts:
*And see if there be any wicked way in me, and lead me in the way everlasting.*

Our Father, who art in Heaven,
*Hallowed be Thy name; Thy kingdom come; Thy will be done in earth as it is in heaven; give us this day our daily bread; and forgive us our trespasses as we forgive them that trespass against us; and lead us not into temptation, but deliver us from evil; for Thine is the kingdom, and the power, and the glory, for ever and ever:*
Amen.

Lord God, Son, Thou Saviour of the world,
*Be gracious unto us.*
By Thy human birth,
By Thy prayers and tears,
By all the troubles of Thy life,
By the grief and anguish of Thy soul,
By Thy bonds and scourgings,
By Thy crown of thorns,
By Thine ignominious crucifixion,
By Thy atoning death,
By Thy rest in the grave,

By Thy glorious resurrection and ascension,
By Thy sitting at the right hand of God,
By Thy divine presence,
By Thy coming again to Thy Church on earth or our being called home to Thee,
*Bless and comfort us, gracious Lord and God.*
Lord God, Holy Ghost,
*Abide with us forever.*

[Then shall all unite in singing the following, or some other suitable hymn.]

T. 595.

A charge to keep I have,
A God to glorify,
A never-dying soul to save,
And fit it for the sky.

Arm me with jealous care,
As in Thy sight to live;
And Oh, Thy servant, Lord, prepare
The strict account to give.

Help me to watch and pray,
And on Thyself rely;
Assured if I my trust betray,
I shall forever die.

[Then may follow a Scripture lesson, and a short address and prayer, after which the Leader shall say, all standing, and repeating together:]

*I believe in the one only God, Father, Son, and Holy Ghost.*

*I believe in God the Father almighty, Maker and Preserver of heaven and earth.*

*I believe in Jesus Christ, the only begotten Son of God, who loved us and gave Himself for us. This is my Lord, who redeemed me, a lost and undone human creature, purchased and gained me from sin, from death and from the power of the devil;*

*Not with gold or silver, but with* His holy **precious blood,** *and with His innocent suffering and dying;*
*To the end that I should be* His own, *and in* **His kingdom** *live under Him and serve Him, in eternal righteousness, innocence, and happiness;*
*So as He, being risen from the dead, liveth and reigneth, world without end.*

*I believe in the Holy Ghost, who proceedeth from the Father and whom our Lord Jesus Christ sent, after He went away, that He should abide with us forever. He calleth me by the gospel, enlighteneth me with His gifts, and preserveth me in the true faith.*

*And the God of peace, that brought again from the dead our Lord Jesus Christ, that great shepherd of the sheep, through the blood of the everlasting covenant, shall also quicken these our mortal bodies, if so be that the spirit of God hath dwell in them.* Amen.

[Then shall all unite in singing:]
The grace of our Lord Jesus Christ,
And the love of God,
And the communion of the Holy Ghost,
Be with us all.
Amen.

---

NO. III.

Te Deum, or T. 22.

From day to day, O Lord, do we
Highly exalt and honor Thee;
Thy name we worship and adore,
World without end, for evermore.

Vouchsafe, O Lord, we humbly pray,
To keep us safe from sin this day,
Lord we have put our trust in Thee,
Confounded let us never be.   Amen.

## OFFICES OF WORSHIP. NO. 3.

Glory be to thee, Lord God our Father,
*Thou Father of mercies, and God of all comfort.*
Thou hast chosen us in Jesus Christ our Lord before the foundation of the world.
*Thou hast delivered us from the power of darkness, and hast translated us into the kingdom of Thy dear Son.*
Thou hast blessed us with all spiritual blessings in heavenly places in Christ;
*Thou hast made us meet to be partakers of the inheritance of the saints in light;*
And hast predestinated us unto the adoption of children to Thyself, according to the good pleasure of Thy will,
*To the praise of the glory of Thy grace, wherein thou hast made us accepted in the Beloved*
Behold, what manner of love the Father has bestowed upon us, that we should be called the sons of God!
*Therefore, with angels and archangels, and with the assembly of just men made perfect, we praise and magnify Thy glorious name!*
Praise, honor, and glory be unto Him, who is Christ, the Son of the living God.
*To Him be glory at all times, in the Church which waiteth for Him, and in that which is about Him,*
From everlasting to everlasting,
Amen.

He is before all things, and by Him all things consist.
*He upholdeth all things by the word of His power, being the brightness of the glory of God and the express image of His person.*
He is the Eternal Word, and was made flesh and dwelt amongst us.
*And they that were His, beheld His glory, the glory of the only begotten of the Father, full of grace and truth.*
In Him dwelleth the whole fulness of the Godhead bodily; He is the true God and eternal life.
*By Himself hath He reconciled all things unto God, whether things on earth, or things in heaven.*

And hath made peace through the blood of His cross.
*Wherefore, God hath highly exalted Him, and given Him a name, which is above every name.*

T. 101. 2 p.

To Him who is, and was, and is to come,
Who died, now ever lives, be praise from every tongue!

Glory be to God, the Holy Ghost, our teacher, guide and comforter!
*Our tongues shall praise Thee, and our lips declare Thy glory.*

O thou most gracious Comforter, who abidest with us forever, we worship Thee with grateful hearts.
*For Thou dost comfort us, as a mother comforteth her children.*

Thou helpest our infirmities and makest intercession for us with groanings which cannot be uttered;
*Thou bearest witness with our spirit, that we are the children of God, and teachest us to cry: Abba, Father!*

Thou sheddest abroad the love of God in the hearts of believers, and makest their bodies Thy holy temples.
*By our own reason or strength we could not believe in nor come to Jesus Christ, our Lord, but Thou callest us and enlightenest us through Thy grace.*

Thou dost sanctify us in the true faith, and wilt enable us to abide in Jesus Christ!
*Be thou praised, together with the Father, and with the Son, now and to all eternity!*

T. 581.

Blessing, honor, glory, might,
And dominion infinite,
To the Father of our Lord,
To the Spirit and the Word;
As it was all worlds before,
Is, and shall be evermore!

OFFICES OF WORSHIP.  NO. 4.    15

[Then may follow a Scripture lesson, and a short address and prayer, at the discretion of the Leader.]

Lord God our Father, who art in Heaven. *Hallowed be Thy name; Thy kingdom come; Thy will be done in earth, as it is in heaven; give us this day our daily bread; and forgive us our trespasses as we forgive them that trespass against us; and lead us not into temptation, but deliver us from evil; for Thine is the kingdom, and the power, and the glory, forever and ever: Amen.*

T. 22.

The grace of our Lord Jesus Christ,
The love of God so highly prized,
The Holy Ghost's communion be,
With all of us most sensibly.

---

## NO. IV.

[The Leader shall say, all standing:]

Lord God, our Father Almighty, Thou art the High and Lofty One that inhabitest eternity; yet Thou dwellest with them also that are of a humble and contrite spirit.

Grant that we may bring unto Thee the sacrifice with which Thou art well pleased, the broken and contrite heart, which Thou, O God, dost not despise.

*We acknowledge our transgressions before Thee. Make us to hear joy and gladness.*

*Hide Thy face from our* **sins and blot out all our transgressions.**

*Create in us a clean heart,* **and renew a right spirit within us.**

*Cast us not away from Thy presence,* **and take not Thy Holy Spirit from us.**

OFFICES OF WORSHIP. NO. 4.

Our Father which art in Heaven,
*Hallowed be Thy name; Thy kingdom come; Thy will be done in earth as it is in heaven; give us this day our daily bread; and forgive us our trespasses as we forgive them that trespass against us; and lead us not into temptation, but deliver us from evil; for Thine is the kingdom, and the power, and the glory, for ever and ever: Amen.*

O Christ, Thou Lamb of God, which takest away the sins of the world,
*Leave Thy peace with us.*
Lord God, Holy Ghost,
*Abide with us forever.*
From the sin of unbelief,
From all defilement of the flesh and spirit,
From every departure from the ways of truth,
From indifference to our soul's salvation,
From every neglect of duty,
From ingratitude and selfishness,
*Preserve us, gracious Lord and God.*
By all the merits of Thy life, sufferings, death and resurrection,
*Bless and save us, O Christ, our Redeemer.*

May Thine early exile
*Teach us to be contented in every place.*

May Thy pure and blameless childhood
*Make us pure in heart and life.*

May Thy love for the sacred Scriptures
*Teach us to prize the word of Truth.*

**May Thy subjection to Thy parents' will**
*Teach us the holy duty of obedience.*

May Thy faithfulness in Thine earthly calling
*Fill us with the spirit of industry and patience.*

May Thy perfect life before God and man
*Incite us to walk in Thy footsteps.*

May Thy tears and agony, Thy crown of thorns and cross,
*Lead us to repentance for our sins.*

May Thy willing sacrifice of Thyself for our salvation,
*Constrain us to dedicate both soul and body to Thy service.*
May Thy atoning death for sin,
*Remain our only hope and joy.*

[Then shall all unite in singing:]

T. 519.

Most Holy Lord and God,
Holy, Almighty God,
Holy and most merciful Saviour,
Thou eternal God!
Grant, that we may never
Lose the comforts from Thy death.
Have mercy, O Lord.

[Then may follow the Scripture lesson, and a short address and prayer, at the discretion of the Leader, after which all shall unite in praying:]

Holy Father, accept us as Thy children in Thy beloved Son, Jesus Christ, who came forth from Thee, and came into the world, was made flesh and dwelt amongst us, took on Him the form of a servant, and hath redeemed us, lost and undone human creatures, from all sin and from death, with His holy and precious blood, and with His innocent suffering and dying; to the end that we should be His own, and in His kingdom live under Him and serve Him, in eternal righteousness, innocence and happiness; forasmuch as He, being risen from the dead, liveth and reigneth, world without end.
Amen.

Blessed be Thou that dwellest between the Cherubim, and graciously regardest them of low estate! O all ye works of the Lord, bless ye the Lord!
*Bless and magnify Him forever!*
Serve the Lord with gladness, and praise His name, for He hath redeemed us from the hand of the enemy, He hath saved us from our sins, and hath delivered us out of many dangers. Praise the Lord for He is good,
*And His mercy endureth forever.*

OFFICES OF WORSHIP. NO. 5.

[Then shall all unite in singing:]

T. 22.

Praise God from whom all blessings flow;
Praise Him, all creatures here below;
Praise Him above, ye heavenly host;
Praise Father, Son, and Holy Ghost.

---

## NO. V.

[The Leader shall say, all standing:]

Blessed are the undefiled in the way, who walk in the law of the Lord. Blessed are they that keep His testimonies, and that seek Him with the whole heart.

*Oh that my ways were directed to keep Thy statutes! Then shall I not be ashamed when I have respect unto Thy commandments.*

My son, forget not my law, but let thine heart keep my commandments; for length of days, and long life and peace shall they add to thee.

*Order my steps in Thy word; and let not any iniquity have dominion over me. Make Thy face to shine upon me, and teach me Thy statutes.*

The statutes of the Lord are right, rejoicing the heart; the commandment of the Lord is pure, enlightening the eyes. The fear of the Lord is clean, enduring for ever; the judgments of the Lord are true and righteous altogether. More to be desired are they than gold, yea, than much fine gold; sweeter also than honey and the honeycomb. Moreover, by them is thy servant warned; and in keeping them there is great reward.

*Hold thou me up, and I shall be safe; and I will have respect unto thy statutes continually.*

[Then shall all unite in singing.]

T. 14.

Let these, oh God, my soul convert,
And make thy servant wise;

Let these be gladness to my heart,
  The day-spring to my eyes.

By these may I be warned betimes;
  Who knows the guile within?
Lord save me from presumptuous crimes,
  Cleanse me from secret sin.

[Then the Leader shall say:]

God spake these words, saying:

[And continuing, the scholars shall repeat after him:]

1. Thou shalt have none other gods before me.
2. Thou shalt not make to thyself any graven image, nor the likeness of any thing that is in heaven above, or in the earth beneath, or in the water under the earth. Thou shalt not bow down to them, nor worship them; for I the Lord thy God am a jealous God, visiting the sins of the fathers upon the children, unto the third and fourth generation of them that hate me; and showing mercy unto thousands of them that love me, and keep my commandments.
3. Thou shalt not take the name of the Lord thy God in vain; for the Lord will not hold him guiltless that taketh His name in vain.
4. Remember the Sabbath day to keep it holy. Six days shalt thou labor, and do all thy work; but the seventh day is the Sabbath of the Lord thy God: in it thou shalt not do any work; thou, nor thy son, nor thy daughter, thy servant, nor thy maid servant, nor thy cattle, nor the stranger that is within thy gates. For in six days the Lord made heaven and earth, the sea and all that in them is, and rested the seventh day; wherefore the Lord blessed the Sabbath day and hallowed it.
5. Honor thy father and thy mother, that thy days may be long in the land which the Lord thy God giveth thee.
6. Thou shalt not kill.
7. Thou shalt not commit adultery.

8. Thou shalt not steal.

9. Thou shalt not bear false witness against thy neighbor.

10. Thou shalt not covet thy neighbor's house, thou shalt not covet thy neighbor's wife, nor his man servant, nor his maid servant, nor his ox, nor his ass, nor any thing that is thy neighbor's.

[Then shall all unite in singing the following, or some other suitable hymn.]

T. 14.

Search me, O God, and know my heart,
Try me, and know each thought;
On me look down in mercy, Lord,
Whom Thou with blood hast bought.

[Here follows the Scripture lesson, and a short address and prayer, at the discretion of the Leader:]

Blessed are the poor in spirit:
*For theirs is the kingdom of Heaven.*

Blessed are they that mourn:
*For they shall be comforted.*

Blessed are the meek:
*For they shall inherit the earth.*

Blessed are they which do hunger and thirst after righteousness:
*For they shall be filled.*

Blessed are the merciful:
*For they shall obtain mercy.*

Blessed are the pure in heart:
*For they shall see God.*

Blessed are the peacemakers:
*For they shall be called the children of God.*

Blessed are they which are persecuted for righteousness' sake:
*For theirs is the kingdom of Heaven.*

Blessed are ye when men shall revile you, and persecute you, and shall say all manner of evil against you falsely, for Christ's sake.

Our Father who art in heaven,
*Hallowed be Thy name; Thy kingdom come; Thy will be done in earth as it is in heaven; give us this day our daily bread; and forgive us our trespasses as we forgive them that trespass against us; and lead us not into temptation, but deliver us from evil; for Thine is the kingdom, and the power, and the glory, for ever and ever:*
Amen.

Then shall all unite in singing:

The grace of our Lord Jesus Christ,
And the love of God,
And the communion of the Holy Ghost,
Be with us all.
Amen.

---

## NO. VI.

[The Leader shall say, all standing:]

God be merciful unto us and bless us;
*And cause His face to shine upon us.*

The Lord is nigh unto them that are of a broken heart;
*And saveth such as be of a contrite spirit.*

How precious are thy thoughts unto me, O God!
*How great is the sum of them!*

If I should count them, they are more in number than the sand;
*When I awake I am still with Thee.*

O, Lord, make clean our hearts within us;
And take not away Thy Holy Spirit from us.

[Then shall all unite in singing:]

T. 36.

Before Thy cross we bow with self-conviction,
Bewail our sins, implore Thy benediction:
For Thou art merciful, and grace unmeasured
In Thee is treasured.

[The part following to the Scripture lesson, may, with great propriety, be prayed kneeling:]

Lord, Lord God, merciful and gracious, long-suffering, and abundant in goodness and truth, keeping mercy for thousands, forgiving iniquity and transgression and sin, and that wilt by no means clear the guilty, against Thee, Thee only have we sinned, and done evil in Thy sight. Forgive us all our transgressions wherein we have transgressed against Thee, and cleanse us from all our sins.

Lord, have mercy upon us.

Remember not, Lord, our offences; spare Thy people, whom Thou hast redeemed with Thy most precious blood, and blot out our sins forever.

Hear us, gracious Lord and God.

From all blindness of heart,
From unbelief and neglect of Thy word,
From irreverence and ingratitude,
From pride, vain-glory, and hypocrisy,
From unholy affections and desires,
From envy, malice, and uncharitableness,
From the power of sin and the snares of the devil,

Deliver us, gracious Lord and God.

By Thy holy birth,
By Thine agony and bloody sweat,

OFFICES OF WORSHIP.  NO. 7.  23

By Thy cross and passion,
By Thy precious death and burial,
By Thy glorious resurrection and ascension,
By Thy sending the Holy Ghost,
By Thy prevailing intercession,
In the hour of death, and in the day of judgment,
*Bless and save us, gracious Lord and God.*

[Here follows the Scripture lesson, and a short address and prayer, at the discretion of the Leader:]

Our Father, who art in heaven,
*Hallowed be Thy name; Thy kingdom come; Thy will be done in earth as it is in heaven; give us this day our daily bread; and forgive us our trespasses as we forgive them that trespass against us; and lead us not into temptation, but deliver us from evil; for Thine is the kingdom, and the power, and the glory, for ever and ever:* Amen.

   The grace of our Lord Jesus Christ,
   And the love of God,
   And the communion of the Holy Ghost,
   Be with us all.
   Amen.

---

## NO. VII.*

[The Leader shall say, all standing:]

It is a good thing to give thanks unto the Lord, and to sing praises unto Thy name, O most High: to show forth Thy loving-kindness in the morning, and Thy faithfulness every night. For Thou, Lord, hast made me glad through Thy work: I will triumph in the works of Thy hands.

*This is the day which the Lord hath made; we will rejoice and be glad in it.*

---

\* For use on the Lord's Day, or, with the omission of the third and fourth sentences, on any festal occasion.

Blessed is the man that keepeth the Sabbath from polluting it, and keepeth his hand from doing any evil.

A day in *Thy courts is better than a thousand; I had rather be a door-keeper in the house of my God, than to dwell in the tents of wickedness.*

The righteous shall flourish like the palm-tree; he shall grow like a cedar in Lebanon. Those that be planted in the house of the Lord shall flourish in the courts of our God.

*We will enter into His gates with thanksgiving, and into His courts with praise.*

O Lord, open Thou our lips;
*And our mouths shall show forth Thy praise.*

[Then shall all unite in singing:]

T. 265 or 11.

Father, God, Thy love we praise,
Love, which gave Thy Son to die:
Jesus, full of truth and grace,
Thee alike we glorify;
Spirit, Comforter divine,
Praise by all to Thee be given,
Till we in full chorus join,
When this earth is changed for heaven.

[Here follows the Scripture lesson, and a short address and prayer, at the discretion of the Leader, after which the Te Deum Laudamus shall be said or chanted.]

We praise Thee, O God; we acknowledge Thee to be the Lord.
*All the earth doth worship Thee,—The Father everlasting.*
To Thee all angels cry aloud,—the heavens and all the powers therein.
*To Thee cherubim and seraphim—continually do cry.*
Holy, holy, holy,—Lord God of Sabaoth;
*Heaven and earth are full—of the majesty of Thy glory.*

The glorious company of the apostles—praise Thee.
*The goodly fellowship of the prophets—praise Thee.*

The noble army of martyrs—praise Thee.
*The holy church throughout all the world doth acknowledge Thee,—the Father of an infinite majesty.*

Thine honorable, true and only Son,—also the Holy Ghost, the Comforter.
*Thou art the King of glory, O Christ;—Thou art the everlasting Son of the Father.*

When Thou tookest upon Thee to deliver man,—Thou didst humble thyself to be born of a virgin.
*When Thou hadst overcome the sharpness of death,—Thou didst open the kingdom of heaven to all believers.*

Thou sittest at the right hand of God,—in the glory of the Father.
*We believe that Thou shalt come—to be our Judge.*

We therefore pray Thee, help Thy servants,—whom Thou hast redeemed with Thy precious blood;
*Make them to be numbered with Thy saints,—in glory everlasting.*

O Lord, save Thy people, and bless Thine heritage:—govern them, and lift them up forever.
*Day by day, we magnify Thee,—and we worship Thy name ever, world without end.*

Vouchsafe, O Lord,—to keep us this day without sin.
*O Lord, have mercy upon us,—have mercy upon us.*

O Lord, let Thy mercy lighten upon us,—as our trust is in Thee.
*O Lord, in Thee have I trusted;—let me never be confounded.*

---

Glory be to the Father, and to the Son,—and to the Holy Ghost;
*As it was in the beginning, is now, and ever shall be—world without end:* Amen.

## NO. VIII.

[From Psalms 139 and 19.]

O Lord, Thou hast searched me and known me.
*Thou knowest my downsitting and mine uprising, Thou understandest my thought afar off.*

Thou compassest my path and my lying down, and art acquainted with all my ways.
*For there is not a word in my tongue, but, lo, O Lord Thou knowest it altogether.*

Thou hast beset me behind and before;
*And laid Thine hand upon me.*

Whither shall I go from Thy spirit?
*Or whither shall I flee from Thy presence?*

If I ascend up into heaven, Thou art there: if I make my bed in hell, behold, Thou art there.
*If I take the wings of the morning, and dwell in the uttermost part of the sea, even there shall Thy hand lead me, and Thy right hand shall hold me.*

If I say, Surely the darkness shall cover me, even the night shall be light about me.
*Yea, the darkness hideth not from Thee, but the night shineth as the day: the darkness and the light are both alike to Thee.*

I will praise Thee, for I am fearfully and wonderfully made.
*Marvellous are Thy works, and that my soul knoweth right well.*

How precious are Thy thoughts unto me, O God! how great is the sum of them.
*If I should count them, they are more in number than the sand: when I awake I am still with Thee.*

Search me, O God, and know my heart; try me, and know my thoughts:
*And see if there be any wicked way in me, and lead me in the way everlasting*

The law of the Lord is perfect, converting the soul: the testimony of the Lord is sure, making wise the simple.

*The statutes of the Lord are right, rejoicing the heart: the commandment of the Lord is pure, enlightening the eyes.*

The fear of the Lord is clean, enduring for ever: the judgments of the Lord are true and righteous altogether.

*More to be desired are they than gold, yea, than much fine gold: sweeter also than honey and the honeycomb.*

Moreover by them is Thy servant warned: and in keeping of them there is great reward.

*Who can understand His errors? Cleanse Thou me from secret faults.*

Keep back Thy servant also from presumptuous sins; let them not have dominion over me.

*Let the words of my mouth, and the meditation of my heart, be acceptable in Thy sight, O Lord, my strength, and my redeemer!*

## IX.

### [From the Epistle to the Romans.]

O Thou, of whom, and through whom, and to whom are all things, help us with one mind and one mouth to glorify Thee, even the Father of our Lord Jesus Christ.

*O Thou, who art the God of hope, fill us with all joy and peace in believing, that we may abound in all hope, through the power of the Holy Ghost.*

May we present our bodies a living sacrifice, holy, acceptable unto Thee, O God, which is our reasonable service. Save us from being conformed to this world; from thinking of ourselves more highly than we ought to think; from being wise in our own conceits; from being overcome of evil, and enable us to overcome evil with good.

*Hear us, and help us, we beseech Thee.*

If we have not liked to retain Thee in our thoughts; if we have despised Thy goodness, forbearance, and long-suffering; if our hearts have been impenitent and hard; if we have dishonored Thee by breaking Thy law;
*Forgive us, we beseech Thee.*

If the good which we would, we do not, and the evil which we would not, that we do; if we find a law in our members warring against the law of our mind, and bringing us into captivity to the law of sin in our members;
*Help us, we beseech Thee, and give us Thy Holy Spirit to keep us safe from sin and the power of the evil one.*

Being justified by faith, may we have peace with Thee, through our Lord Jesus Christ, and rejoice in the hope of the glory of God.
*Shed Thy love in our hearts by the Holy Ghost.*

May the law of the Spirit of life in Christ Jesus make us free from the law of sin and death, and make us walk not after the flesh, but after the spirit; may we not receive the spirit of bondage again to fear, but the spirit of adoption, whereby we call Thee Father.
*Being led by the Spirit, may we become Thy children.*

May nothing separate us from the love of Christ; neither tribulation, nor distress, nor persecution, nor famine, nor nakedness, nor peril, nor sword;
*In all these may we be more than conquerors through Him that loved us.*

May neither death nor life, nor angels nor powers, nor things present nor things to come, nor height nor depth, nor any other creature, separate us from the love of God which is in Christ Jesus.
*May nothing separate us from Thy love.*

May we confess with our mouth the Lord Jesus, and believe in our heart that God has raised Him from the dead.
*May we believe with our heart unto righteousness, and confess with our mouth unto salvation.*

May our love be without dissimulation; may we abhor that which is evil, and cleave to that which is good; be kindly affectioned one toward another; not slothful in business, fervent in spirit, serving the Lord; continuing instant in **prayer**; recompensing to none evil for evil; providing **things** honest in the sight of all men; casting off the **works** of darkness, and putting on the armor of light.

*Whether we live, may we live unto the Lord; and whether we die, may we die unto the Lord.*

Now unto Him that hath power to establish us according to the Gospel, and the preaching of Jesus Christ,

*To God only wise, be glory through Jesus Christ for ever. Amen.*

---

## NO. X.

### [From the Epistle to the Ephesians.]

O Thou, who art the one God and Father of all; who art above all, and through all, and in us all; who hast adopted us as children in Jesus Christ, Thy Son, in whom we have redemption, even the forgiveness of our sins; quicken us, we beseech Thee, who have been dead in trespasses and sins.

*For the sake of Thy great love wherewith Thou hast loved us, make us alive in Christ.*

Give us, we beseech Thee, the spirit of wisdom and revelation in the knowledge of Thyself, that we may know the hope of Thy calling and the riches of Thine inheritance, and the exceeding greatness of Thy power, which Thou hast wrought in Christ, when Thou didst raise Him from the dead, and set Him at Thine own right hand in heavenly places.

*We pray Thee to raise us up also, and make us to sit in heavenly places with Him.*

May we be strengthened with might by Thy Spirit in the inner man, that Christ may dwell in our hearts by faith; that, being rooted and grounded in love, we may be able to comprehend the breadth and length, and depth and height, of the love of Christ, and be filled with all the fulness of God.

*Help us to come in the unity of the faith, and the knowledge of the Son of God, to the stature of a perfect man, to the measure of the fulness of Christ.*

May we conduct ourselves with all lowliness and meekness, with long-suffering, forbearing one another in love, putting away all bitterness, and wrath, and anger, and evil-speaking, with all malice.

*May we be kind one to another, tender-hearted, forgiving one another, even as God for Christ's sake hath forgiven us.*

May we be followers of Thee, as dear children, and walk in love, as Christ hath loved us; redeeming the time; having the fruit of the Spirit in all goodness, and righteousness and peace.

*May we give thanks, always, for all things, unto God the Father, in the name of our Lord Jesus Christ.*

Help us to pray always, with all prayer and supplication in the Spirit,

*And watching thereunto with all perseverance.*

Grace be with all them that love our Lord Jesus Christ in sincerity.

Amen.

## NO. XI.

### [From the Epistles of James and John.]

O God, the Father of lights, with whom there is no variableness nor shadow of turning, from whom cometh every good and perfect gift, we ask of Thee wisdom, who givest to all men liberally and upbraidest not.

*We would ask in faith, nothing wavering; believing that, if we draw nigh to Thee, Thou wilt draw nigh to us.*

O Lord, who canst not be tempted with evil, neither canst tempt any man, we confess that we are drawn away by our own lusts and enticed; but we beseech Thee, who art very pitiful and of tender mercy, who dost resist the proud, but givest grace to the humble, to hear the prayer of faith and raise us up.

*If we have known to do good and done it not; if we have been hearers of the word, and not doers also, deceiving our own selves: forgive us, and save us, we beseech Thee.*

Give us, O Lord, the wisdom from above, which is first pure, then peaceable, gentle, easy to be entreated, full of mercy and good fruits, without partiality, and without hypocrisy.

*O Thou, who art light, and in whom is no darkness at all, may we walk in light, and have fellowship with Thee.*

O Thou, who art love, may we dwell in love, and so dwell in Thee: may our love be made perfect, and be free from all fear; may we be born of God, and overcome the world; may we keep Thy commandments, and love Thy children.

*May we love Thee, not in word and tongue, but in deed and truth, and hereby know that we are of the truth, and assure our hearts before Thee.*

May we not love the world, nor the things which are in the world; may we remember that the world passeth away, and the lust thereof, and that if we love the world, the love of the Father is not in us.

*May we grow in grace and in the knowledge of our Lord and Saviour Jesus Christ.*

To Him be glory, both now and forever.
Amen.

# HYMNS.

### THE WORD OF GOD.

**1.**  T. 119.

Thanks and praise, :||:
Thanks and praise be ever Thine,
That Thy word to us is given,
Teaching us with power divine,
That the Lord of earth and heaven,
Everlasting life for us to gain,
Once was slain. :||:

2. Lord, our God, :||:
May Thy precious saving word,
Till our race is here completed,
Light unto our path afford;
And when in Thy presence seated,
We to Thee will render for Thy grace
Ceaseless praise. :||:

Gregor.

L. M.  **2.**  T. 22. g.

'Twas by an order from the Lord,
The ancient prophets spoke His word;
His Spirit did their tongues inspire,
And warm'd their heart with heavenly fire.

2. O God, mine eyes with pleasure look
On the dear volume of Thy book;
There my Redeemer's face I see,
And read His name, who died for me.

## THE WORD OF GOD.

3. Let the false raptures of the mind
Be lost and vanish in the wind;
Here I can fix my hope secure;
This is Thy word and must endure.

*Watts.*

C. M.     **3.**     T. 593 or 14.

How precious is the Book divine,
  By inspiration given;
Bright as a lamp its doctrines shine,
  To guide our souls to heaven.

2. It sweetly cheers our drooping hearts,
  In this dark vale of tears;
Life, light, and joy it still imparts,
  And quells our rising fears.

3. This lamp thro' all the tedious night
  Of life shall guide our way,
Till we behold the clearer light
  Of everlasting day.

*Fawcett.*

C. M.     **4.**     T. 14.

Thy law is perfect, Lord of light,
  Thy testimonies sure;
The statutes of Thy realm are right,
  And Thy commandments pure.

2. Holy, inviolate Thy fear,
  Enduring as Thy throne;
Thy judgments, chastening or severe,
  Justice and truth alone.

3. More prized than gold,—than gold whose waste
  Refining fire expels:
Sweeter than honey to my taste,
  Than honey from the cells.

4. Let these, O God, my soul convert,
    And make Thy servant wise;
Let these be gladness to my heart,
    The day-spring to my eyes.

5. By these may I be warn'd betimes;
    Who knows the guile within?
Lord, save me from presumptuous crimes,
    Cleanse me from secret sin.

6. So may the words my lips express,
    The thoughts that throng my mind,
O Lord, my strength and righteousness,
    With Thee acceptance find.

Montgomery.

11 s.       **5.**       T. 39.

The Bible! the Bible! more precious than gold
The hopes and the glories its pages unfold;
It speaks of a Saviour and tells of His Love;
It shows us the way to the mansions above.

2. The Bible! the Bible! blest volume of truth,
How sweetly it smiles on the season of youth!
It bids us seek early the pearl of great price,
Ere the heart is enslaved in the bondage of vice.

3. The Bible! the Bible! we hail it with joy,
Its truths and its glories our tongues shall employ;
We'll sing of its triumphs, we'll tell of its worth,
And send its glad tidings afar o'er the earth.

4. The Bible! the Bible! the valleys shall ring,
And hill-tops re-echo the notes that we sing;
Our banner, inscribed with its precepts and rules,
Shall long wave in triumph, the joy of our schools.

THE WORD OF GOD.

C. M.

**6.**

T. 14. a.

Laden with guilt, and full of fears
  I fly to Thee, my Lord;
And not a ray of hope appears,
  But in Thy written word.

2. The volume of my Father's grace
  Does all my grief assuage;
Here I behold my Saviour's face
  In almost every page.

3. This is the field where hidden lies
  The pearl of price unknown;
That merchant is divinely wise
  Who makes the pearl his own.

4. This is the judge that ends the strife
  Where wit and reason fail;
My guide to everlasting life
  Through all this gloomy vale.

Watts.

8s. & 7s.

**7.**

T. 16.

What a mercy, what a treasure
  We possess in God's own word,
Where we read with sacred pleasure
  Of the love of Christ our Lord.

2. That blest word reveals the Saviour,
  Whom our souls so deeply need;
O what mercy, love and favor,
  That for sinners Christ should bleed.

3. While each wretched heathen nation
  Nothing knows, dear Lord, of Thee,
In this happy land, Salvation
  Clearly is revealed to me.

CREATION AND PROVIDENCE.

4. O the blessedness of knowing
Christ our Saviour's precious love,
Freely on a child bestowing
Grace and mercy from above.

L. M.　　　　　**8.**　　　　　T. 22.

With humble prayer, oh, may I read
Whate'er shall to my Saviour lead;
Lord, send Thy Spirit to impart
A wise and understanding heart.

2. Be Thou my Teacher, Thou my Guide;
May all I read be well applied;
My danger and my refuge show,
And let me Thy salvation know.

---

## CREATION AND PROVIDENCE.

L. M.　　　　　**9.**　　　　　T. 22.

Give to our God immortal praise;
Mercy and truth are all His ways:
Wonders of grace to God belong,
Repeat His mercies in your song.

2. Give to the Lord of lords renown,
The King of kings with glory crown;
His mercies ever shall endure,
When earth-born powers are known no more.

3. He built the earth, He spread the sky,
And fix'd the starry lights on high:
Wonders of grace to God belong,
Repeat His mercies in your song.

CREATION AND PROVIDENCE.

4. He fills the sun with morning light,
He bids the moon direct the night:
His mercies ever shall endure,
When suns and moons shall shine no more.

5. He sent His Son with power to save
From guilt, from darkness, and the grave:
Wonders of grace to God belong,
Repeat His mercies in your song.

6. Thro' this vain world He guides our feet,
And leads us to His heavenly seat:
His mercies ever shall endure,
When this vain world shall be no more.

Watts

C. M.
## 10.
T. 593. a.

I sing the almighty power of God,
  That made the mountains rise;
That spread the flowing seas abroad,
  And built the lofty skies.

2. I sing the wisdom that ordained
  The sun to rule the day:
The moon shines full at His command,
  And all the stars obey.

3. I sing the goodness of the Lord,
  That filled the earth with food:
He formed the creatures with His word,
  And then pronounced them good.

4. Lord, how Thy wonders are displayed,
  Where'er I turn mine eyes,
Though I survey the ground I tread,
  Or gaze upon the skies!

5. There's not a plant or flower below,
  But makes Thy glories known;
And clouds arise, and tempests blow,
  By order from Thy throne.

Watts.

## CREATION AND PROVIDENCE.

**11.**

L. M. (Double.)  T. 166.

High in the heavens, eternal God,
Thy goodness in full glory shines;
Thy truth shall break thro' every cloud
That veils and darkens Thy designs.
Forever firm Thy justice stands,
As mountains their foundations keep;
Great are the wonders of Thy hands;
Thy judgments are a mighty deep.

2. Thy providence is kind and large,
Both man and beast Thy bounty share;
The whole creation is Thy charge,
But man is Thy peculiar care.
My God, how excellent Thy grace!
Whence all our hope and comfort springs;
The sons of Adam in distress
Fly to the shadow of Thy wings.

3. From the provisions of Thy house
We shall be fed with sweet repast;
There mercy like a river flows,
And we the living water taste:
Life, like a fountain rich and free,
Springs from Thy presence, gracious Lord;
And in Thy light our souls shall see
The glories promis'd in Thy word.

Watts.

**12.**

7s. & 6s.  T. 151.

Children of God lack nothing,
  His promise bears them thro';
Who gives the lilies clothing,
  Will clothe His people too:
Beneath the spreading heavens,
  No creature but is fed;
And He who feeds the ravens,
  Will give His children bread.

2. Tho' vine, nor fig-tree neither,
   Their wonted fruit should bear;
Though all the field should wither,
   Nor flocks nor herds be there:
Yet God the same abiding,
   His praise shall tune my voice;
For, while in Him confiding,
   I cannot but rejoice.

*Newton.*

## 13.

7s.  T. 581 or 83.

Quiet, Lord, my froward heart,
   Make me teachable and mild,
Upright, simple, free from art,
   Make me as a weaned child;
From distrust and envy free,
Pleas'd with all that pleaseth Thee.

2. What Thou shalt to-day provide,
   Let me as a child receive;
What to-morrow may betide,
   Calmly to Thy wisdom leave:
'Tis enough that Thou wilt care,
Why should I the burden bear?

3. As a little child relies
   On a care beyond his own,
Knows he's neither strong nor wise,
   Fears to stir a step alone:
Let me thus with Thee abide,
As my Father, Guard, and Guide.

4. Thus preserv'd from Satan's wiles,
   Safe from dangers, free from fears,
May I live upon Thy smiles,
   Till the promised hour appears,
When the sons of God shall prove
All their Father's boundless love.

*Newton.*

## CREATION AND PROVIDENCE.

C. M.

### 14.

T. 14.

God moves in a mysterious way,
  His wonders to perform;
He plants His footsteps in the sea,
  And rides upon the storm.

2. Deep in unfathomable mines
    Of never-failing skill
  He treasures up His bright designs,
    And works His sovereign will.

3. Ye fearful saints, fresh courage take;
    The clouds you so much dread
  Are big with mercy, and shall break
    In blessings on your head.

4. Judge not the Lord by feeble sense,
    But trust Him for His grace;
  Behind a frowning providence
    He hides a smiling face.

5. His purposes will ripen fast,
    Unfolding every hour:
  The bud may have a bitter taste,
    But sweet will be the flower.

6. Blind unbelief is sure to err,
    And scan His work in vain;
  God is His own interpreter,
    And He will make it plain.

Cowper.

### 15.

T. 132. D.

All glory to the sovereign Good,
And Father of compassion,
To God, our help and sure abode,
Whose gracious visitation
Renews His blessings every day,

And takes our griefs and fears away,
Give to our God the glory.

2. What is created by our God
Enjoys His preservation;
And He extends o'er all abroad
His fatherly compassion:
Throughout the kingdom of His grace
Prevail His truth and righteousness:
Give to our God the glory.

3. As long as I have breath in me
I will sound forth His praises;
His precious saving name shall be
Exalted in all places:
My heart, with all thy strength adore
The God of grace, the God of power,
And give Him all the glory.

J. J. Schultz.

## 16.

Day by day the manna fell;
Oh, to learn this lesson well!
Still by constant mercy fed,
Give me, Lord, my daily bread.

2. Day by day the promise reads,
Daily strength for daily needs,
Cast foreboding fears away:
Take the manna of to-day.

3. Lord, my times are in Thy hand;
All my brightest hopes have planned
To Thy wisdom I resign,
And would make Thy purpose mine.

4. Thou my daily task shalt give;
Day by day to Thee I live:
So shall added years fulfill,
Not my own—my Father's will.

Condor.

## 17.

### The Ministry of Angels.
#### Hebrews i. 14.   Matt. xviii. 10.

Angels, where'er we go, attend
  Our steps, whate'er betide;
With watchful care their charge defend,
  And evil turn aside.

2. Myriads of bright cherubic bands,
  Sent by the King of kings,
Rejoice to bear us in their hands,
  And shade us with their wings.

3. Jehovah's charioteers surround;
  The ministerial choir
Encamp where'er His heirs are found,
  And form our wall of fire.

4. Ten thousand offices unseen
  For us they gladly do,
Deliver in the furnace keen,
  And safe escort us through.

5. And thronging round, with steadfast love,
  They guard the dying breast,
The lurking fiend far off remove,
  And soothe our souls to rest.

6. And when our spirits we resign,
  On outstretched wings they bear,
And lodge us in the arms Divine,
  And leave us ever there.

                Wesley.

## REDEMPTION.
### Titus ii. 14.

C. M.

### 18.

T. 14.

Plunged in a gulf of dark despair,
  We wretched sinners lay,
Without one cheerful beam of hope,
  Or spark of glimmering day.

2. With pitying eyes the Prince of grace
    Beheld our helpless grief;
  He saw, and—O amazing love!—
    He ran to our relief.

3. Down from the shining seats above,
    With joyful haste He fled,
  Entered the grave in mortal flesh,
    And dwelt among the dead.

4. O for this love let rocks and hills
    Their lasting silence break;
  And all harmonious human tongues
    The Saviour's praises speak.

*Watts.*

C. M.

### 19.

T. 14. or 593.

O for a thousand tongues to sing
  My dear Redeemer's praise;
The glories of my God and King,
  The triumphs of His grace.

2. Jesus, the name that charms our fears,
    That bids our sorrows cease:
  'Tis music in the sinner's ears,
    'Tis life, and health, and peace.

3. His grace subdues the power of sin,
    He sets the prisoner free;
  His blood can make the foulest clean,
    His blood avail'd for me.

4. He speaks, and listening to His voice
   New life the dead receive:
The mournful, broken hearts rejoice,
   The humble poor believe.

5. Hear Him, ye deaf; His praise, ye dumb,
   Your loosen'd tongues employ;
Ye blind, behold your Saviour come;
   And leap, ye lame, for joy.

6. Look unto Him, ye nations, own
   Your God, ye fallen race:
Look and be sav'd through faith alone,
   Be justified by grace.
                                    C. Wesley.

## 20.

12s.*                                T. 39.

The voice of free grace cries escape to the mountain,
For Adam's lost race Christ hath opened a fountain,
For sin and uncleanness and every transgression,
His blood flows most freely in streams of salvation.
               (CHORUS.
Hallelujah to the Lamb! He hath bought us our pardon,
We'll praise Him again when we pass over Jordan.)

2. Ye souls that are wounded! O flee to the Saviour;
He calls you in mercy,—'tis infinite favor;
Tho' your sins be as scarlet,—escape to the mountain,—
That blood can remove them, which flows from this fountain.

3. O Jesus! ride onward, triumphantly glorious;
O'er sin, death and hell Thou'rt more than victorious;
Thy name is the theme of the great congregation,
While angels and men raise the shout of salvation.

4. With joy shall we stand when escaped to that shore;
With our harps in our hands we will praise Him the more;
We'll range the sweet plains on the banks of the river,
And sing of salvation for ever and ever.        Thornby.

        * Plym. Coll., p. 379.

### 21.

T. 79.

Thou holy, spotless Lamb of God,
Didst leave Thy glorious, blest abode,
  In love to sinners vile;
Earth's face the curse had overrun,
Man was corrupt, condemn'd, undone,
  Entangled fast by Satan's guile.

2. Thou, for their sake who hated Thee,
Didst shed Thy blood upon the tree,
  Thy life for ours didst give;
Thou barest our curse; our debt was paid;
Thy soul for sin an offering made;
  Thou diedst that we with Thee might live.

3. Never may we depart from Thee;
Thou hast procur'd our liberty,
  Thanks to Thy boundless grace.
Thy cross, whereon our sins were nailed,
Our refuge be from sin and death,
  Our feeble soul's abiding-place.

M. Taylor.

### 22.

T. 586.

I will rejoice in God my Saviour,
And magnify this act of love;
I'm lost in wonder at His favor,
Which made Him leave His throne above,
To take upon Him human nature,
To suffer for His wretched creature,
Dire anguish, keenest pain,
And death-pangs to sustain,
  My soul to gain.

Benj. Latrobe.

## THE COMING OF CHRIST.
*Advent.*
Isa. lxi. 1; Rom. xiii. 12.

**23.**

C M.                                                                 T. 14.

Hark, the glad sound! the Saviour comes,
The Saviour promis'd long;
Let every heart prepare a throne,
And every voice a song.

2. He comes, the prisoners to release,
In Satan's bondage held;
The gates of brass before him burst,
The iron fetters yield.

3. He comes, from thickest films of vice,
To clear the mental ray,
And on the eye, long clos'd in night,
To pour celestial day.

4. He comes, the broken heart to bind,
The bleeding soul to cure;
And with the riches of His grace
To bless the humble poor.

5. Our glad hosannas, Prince of Peace,
Thy welcome shall proclaim;
And heaven's eternal arches ring
With Thy beloved name!

Doddridge.

**24.**

7s. & 6s.                                                            T. 151. g.

How shall I meet my Saviour?
  How shall I welcome Thee?
What manner of behavior
  Is now required of me?
I wait for Thy salvation,
  Grant me Thy Spirit's light,
Thus will my preparation
  Be pleasing in Thy sight.

ADVENT.

2. While with her sweetest flowers
   Thy Zion strews Thy way,
I'll raise with all my powers
   To Thee a grateful lay:
To Thee, the King of Glory,
   I'll tune a song divine,
And make Thy love's bright story
   In graceful numbers shine.

3. No sinful man's endeavor,
   Nor any mortal's care,
Could draw His sovereign favor
   To sinners in despair:
Uncall'd He comes with gladness
   Us from the fall to raise,
And change our grief and sadness
   To songs of joy and praise.

P. Gerhard.

## 25.

L. M.                                                       T. 22. b.

Hosanna to the living Lord!
Hosanna to th' incarnate Word!
To Christ, Creator, Saviour, King,
Let earth, let heaven, Hosanna sing!

2. Hosanna, Lord! Thine angels cry;
Hosanna, Lord! Thy saints reply;
Above, beneath us, and around,
The dead and living swell the sound.

3. O Saviour! with protecting care,
Return to this Thy house of prayer;
Assembled in Thy sacred name,
Here we Thy parting promise claim.

4. But, chiefest, in our cleansed breast,
Eternal! bid Thy Spirit rest,
And make our secret soul to be
A temple pure, and worthy Thee!

## THE SECOND COMING OF CHRIST. 49

5. So, in the last and dreadful day,
When earth and heaven shall melt away,
Thy flock, redeemed from sinful stain,
Shall swell the sound of praise again.

*Heber.*

L. M. **26.** T. 22.

On Jordan's banks the Baptist's cry
Announces that the Lord is nigh:
Come near and hearken, for He brings
Glad tidings from the King of kings.

2. Be purified each Christian breast,
And furnish'd for so great a guest:
Yea, let us all our hearts prepare
For Christ to come and enter there.

3. For Thou art our Salvation, Lord,
Our Refuge and our great Reward;
Without Thy grace our souls must fade,
And wither like a flower decay'd.

4. Stretch forth Thine hand a balm to pour,
And make us rise to fall no more:
Upon Thy pardoned people shine,
And fill the world with grace divine.

*From the Latin.*

8s, 7s & 4s. **27.** T. 585.

*Christ's Second Coming.*

Lo, He cometh! countless trumpets
Christ's appearance usher in:
'Midst ten thousand saints and angels
See our Judge and Saviour shine:
　Hallelujah! :||:
Welcome, welcome, Lamb once slain!

ADVENT.

2. Now the song of all the saved,
"Worthy is the Lamb," resounds:
Now resplendent shine His nail-prints,
Every eye shall see His wounds:
   Great His glory; :||:
Every knee to Him shall bow.

3. Every island, sea, and mountain,
Earth and heaven flee away;
All His enemies confounded
Hear the trump proclaim His day:
   Come to judgment, :||:
Stand before the Son of Man.

4. All who love Him view His glory
In His bright, once marred face:
Jesus cometh; all His people
Now their heads with gladness raise:
   Happy mourners, :||:
Lo, on clouds He comes, He comes!

5. See redemption, long expected,
On that awful day appear;
All His people, once despised,
Joyful meet Him in the air:
   Hallelujah, :||:
Saviour, now Thy kingdom comes!

*Cennick.*

S. M.  **28.**  T. 582.

And will the Judge descend?
   And must the dead arise,
And not a single soul escape
   His all discerning eyes?

2. How will my heart endure
   The terrors of that day,
When earth and heaven before His face,
   Astonished, shrink away?

3. But ere the trumpet shakes
   The mansions of the dead,
Hark! from the Gospel's cheering sound,
   What joyful tidings spread!

4. Ye sinners, seek His grace
   Whose wrath ye cannot bear;
Fly to the shelter of His cross,
   And find salvation there.

*Doddridge.*

## THE BIRTH OF CHRIST.

*Christmas.*

Is. ix. 6.   John i. 14.

### 29.

7s.   T. 11.

What good news the angels bring!
What glad tidings of our King!
Christ the Lord is born to-day,
Christ, who takes our sins away!

2. He who rules both heaven and earth
Hath in Bethlehem His birth;
Him shall all the faithful see,
And rejoice eternally.

3. Lift your hearts and voices high,
With hosannas fill the sky:
Glory be to God above,
Who is infinite in love!

4. Peace on earth, good will to men!
Now with us our God is seen:
Angels join His name to praise,
Help to sing redeeming grace.

5. Jesus is the loveliest name,
This the angel doth proclaim;

CHRISTMAS.

Sinners poor He came to save,
They in Him redemption have.

6. They who see themselves undone,
And take refuge to the Son,
They shall all be born again,
And with Him in glory reign.

Hammond.

7s.

## 30.

T 11. a.

All the world give praises due;
God is faithful, God is true;
He to man doth comfort send
In His Son, the sinner's friend.

2. What the fathers wish'd of old,
What the promises foretold,
What the seers did prophesy,
Is fulfilled most gloriously.

3. My salvation, welcome be!
Thou, my portion, praise to Thee!
Come and make Thy blest abode
In my heart, O Son of God!

4. Grant Thy comforts to my mind,
Since I'm helpless, poor, and blind;
O may I in faith abide
Thine, and never turn aside.

5. Jesus, when in majesty
Thou shalt come my judge to be,
Grant in grace that I may stand
Justified at Thy right hand.

H. Held.

L. M.

## 31.

T. 22. b.

Immanuel, to Thee we sing,
Thou Prince of Life, almighty King,
That Thou, expected ages past,
Didst come to visit us at last.

THE BIRTH OF CHRIST. 53

2. Thou, Lord, tho' heaven belongs to Thee,
On earth a stranger deign'st to be;
Thou clothest all, yet wear'st a dress
Which doth the poorest state express.

3. On wither'd grass reclines Thy head,
A wretched manger is Thy bed:
Tho' Thou appear'st among Thine own,
No kindness unto Thee is shown.

4. I thank Thee, gracious Lord, that Thou
On my account did'st stoop so low;
O that my words, my works and ways,
May all proclaim Thy matchless praise.
                                            Gerhard.

8s. & 7s.*            **32.**            T. 16.

Christ the Lord, the Lord most glorious,
  Now is born; O shout aloud!
Man by Him is made victorious:
  Praise your Saviour, hail your God!
    (*Chorus.* Hail, hail this happy day.)

2. Praise the Lord, for on us shineth
    Christ, the Sun of righteousness;
  He to us in love inclineth,
    Cheers our souls with pardoning grace.
      (*Chorus.*)

3. Praise the Lord, whose saving splendor
    Shines into the darkest night;
  O what praises shall we render
    For this never-ceasing light.
      (*Chorus.*)

4. Praise the Lord God, our salvation,
    Praise Him who retriev'd our loss;
  Sing with awe, and love's sensation,
    HALLELUJAH, GOD WITH US.
      (*Chorus.*)                      J. Miller.

\* Golden Chain, p. 96.

CHRISTMAS.

8s. 7s. & 4s.  **33.**  T. 585.

Hail, thou wondrous infant stranger
  Born lost Eden to regain;
Welcome in Thy humble manger,
  Welcome to Thy creature man;
    Hail Immanuel, :‖:
Thou who wast ere time began.

2. Say, ye blest seraphic legions,
  What thus brought your Maker down?
Say, why did He leave your regions,
  Why forsake His heavenly throne?
    Notes melodious :‖:
Tell the cause: Good will to man.

3. We this offer'd Saviour needed,
  Hence we join your theme with joy.
We by none will be exceeded,
  While we laud this mystery,
    And with wonder :‖:
God incarnate glorify.

8s. 7s. & 4s.  **34.**  T. 585.

Angels, from the realms of glory
Wing your flight o'er all the earth,
Ye who sang creation's story,
Now proclaim Messiah's birth:
    Come and worship, :‖:
Worship Christ, the new born King.

2. Shepherds, in the field abiding,
Watching o'er your flocks by night,
God with man is now residing,
Yonder shines the infant-light:
    Come and worship, :‖:
Worship Christ, the new born King.

## THE BIRTH OF CHRIST.

3. Sages, leave your contemplations,
Brighter visions beam afar;
Seek the great Desire of nations;
Ye have seen His natal star:
    Come and worship, :‖:
Worship Christ, the new born King.

4. Saints, before the altar bending,
Watching long in hope and fear,
Suddenly the Lord descending,
In His temple shall appear:
    Come and worship, :‖:
Worship Christ, the new born King.

5. Sinners, wrung with true repentance,
Doom'd for guilt to endless pains,
Justice now revokes the sentence,
Mercy calls you,—break your chains:
    Come and worship, :‖:
Worship Christ, the new born King.
Montgomery.

## 35.   T. 11. a.

Hark! the herald angels sing:
"Glory to the new born King!
Glory in the highest heaven,
Peace on earth, and man forgiv'n."

2. Joyful, all ye nations, rise;
Join the triumph of the skies:
With th angelic host proclaim:
"Christ is born in Bethlehem!"

3. Veil'd in flesh the Godhead see!
Hail the incarnate Deity!
Pleas'd as man with men to dwell,
Jesus our Immanuel.

CHRISTMAS.

4. Hail the heaven-born Prince of Peace!
Hail, the Sun of Righteousness!
Light and life to all He brings,
Ris'n with healing in His wings.

5. Lo, He lays His glory by!
Born that man no more may die;
Born to raise the sons of earth;
Born to give them second birth.

6. Sing we, then, with angels sing:
"Glory to the new-born King!
Glory in the highest heaven,
Peace on earth, and man forgiv'n."

C. Wesley

## 36.

7s             T. 11

Sweeter sounds than music knows
  Charm me in Immanuel's name;
All her hopes my spirit owes
  To His birth, and cross, and shame.

2. When He came the angels sung,
  "Glory be to God on high!"
Lord, unloose my stammering tongue,
  Who should louder sing than I?

3. Did the Lord a man become,
  That He might the law fulfill,
Bleed and suffer in my room,
  And canst thou, my tongue, be still?

4. No, I must my praises bring,
  Though they worthless are and weak
For should I refuse to sing,
  Sure the very stones would speak.

5. O my Saviour, Shield, and Sun,
  Shepherd, Brother, Husband, Friend,
Ev'ry precious name in one,
  I will love Thee without end.

Newton.

## THE BIRTH OF CHRIST.

7s.

### 37.
T. 11.

Bright and joyful is the morn,
For to us a child is born;
From the highest realms of heaven
Unto us a Son is given.

2. On His shoulder He shall bear
Power and majesty, and wear
On His vesture and His thigh
Names most awful, names most high.

3. Wonderful in counsel He,
Christ, th' incarnate Deity,
Sire of ages ne'er to cease,
King of kings, and Prince of Peace.

4. Come and worship at His feet;
Yield to Him the homage meet;
From the manger to the throne,
Homage due to God alone.

*Montgomery.*

8s. & 7s.*

### 38.
T. 16.

Hark! what mean those holy voices,
　Sweetly sounding through the skies?
Lo! th'angelic host rejoices,
　Heavenly hallelujahs rise.

2. Hear them tell the wondrous story,
　Hear them chant in hymns of joy:—
"Glory in the highest, glory!
　Glory be to God most high!

3. "Peace on earth, good-will from heaven,
　Reaching far as man is found;
Souls redeemed, and sins forgiven!—
　Loud our golden harps shall sound.

\* Plym. Coll. p. 64.

CHRISTMAS.

4. "Christ is born, the great Anointed;
   Heaven and earth His praises sing!
 O receive whom God appointed
   For your Prophet, Priest and King!

5. "Haste, ye mortals, to adore Him;
   Learn His name, and taste His joy;
 Till in heaven ye sing before Him,—
   Glory be to God most high!"

Cawood.

P. M.*
## 39.

There's a song the angels sing,
  And its notes with rapture ring,
Round the throne whose radiance fills the heavens above.
  Shepherds heard the distant strain,
  Watching on Judea's plain,
"Glory be to God, to men be peace and love."
  CHORUS.
  Through the earth and through the sky,
  Let the anthem ever fly,
"Glory be to God again, peace on earth, good-will to men."

2. 'Tis a song for children too;
   To the Saviour 'tis their due;
 Let its grateful notes ascend to Him again;
   Join with angels in their song,
   And the heavenly strain prolong,
 "Glory be to God, good-will and peace to men."
   CHORUS.  Through the earth, &c.

3. Soon around that throne may we
   With those happy angels be,
 Striking harps to strains that never more shall cease:
   Mingling love with loftiest praise,
   Still the chorus there we'll raise,
 "Glory be to God, to men good will and peace."
   CHORUS.  Through the earth, &c.

* Golden Chain, p. 114.

## 40.

P. M.*

Hark the angels singing, wake the happy morn,
Joyful tidings bringing, "Christ, the Lord, is born.
In a lowly manger (this shall be the sign),
See the new born stranger, hail the babe divine."

### Chorus.

Glory! glory! glory! In the highest sing!
Glory! glory! glory! To our God and King!
Glory! glory! glory! Peace to earth again!
Glory! glory! glory! And good-will to men!

2. Sisters dear, and brothers, sing, sing away!
This of all the others, is the children's day!
Hear the blessed story, "once as young as we,
Christ the Prince of glory, slept on Mary's knee."
    Glory! &c.

3. Where's a chorus meeter for His advent here?
Where a carol sweeter, to His gentle ear?
None can come so near Him, th' Holy, Undefiled,
None so love and fear Him, as a Christian child.
    Glory! &c.

4. In the highest regions, now upon His throne,
All the blood-bought legions claim Him Lord alone:
But of all wh' adore Him, with triumphant song,
Children stand before Him in the greatest throng.
    Glory! &c.

5. Let us then pursue Him, to His throne of grace;
Let us pray unto Him, looking in His face:
"Once in chilhood's weakness, Christ, like us, wert Thou;
In love, truth and meekness, make us like Thee now."
    Glory! &c.

* S. S. Bell, p. 58.

6. This, of all the others, is the children's day,
Sisters dear, and brothers, sing, sing away,
Bless Him for its story: "once as young as we,
Jesus, Lord of glory, slept on Mary's knee."
    Glory! &c.

P. M.

## 41.

T. 151.

Softly the night is sleeping
  On Bethlehem's peaceful hill;
Silent the shepherds watching,
  The gentle flocks are still.
But hark! the wondrous music
  Falls from the opening sky;
Valley and cliff re-echo
  Glory to God on high!

    (CHORUS.
  Glory to God! it rings again,
  Peace on earth! good will to men!)

2. Day in the East is breaking;
    Day o'er the crimsoned earth;
  Now the glad world is waking,
    Glad in the Saviour's birth!
  See where the clear star bendeth
    Over the manger blest:
  See, where the infant Jesus
    Smiles upon Mary's breast!

    (CHORUS.
  Glory to God!—we hear again;
  Peace on earth! good will to men!)

3. Come with the gladsome shepherds,
    Quick hastening from the fold;
  Come with the wise men, pouring
    Incense and myrrh and gold.

## THE EPIPHANY.

Come to Him, poor and lowly,
  Around the cradle throng;
Come with your hearts of sunshine,
  And sing the angels' song.
    (CHORUS.
  Glory to God!—tell out again;
  Peace on earth! good will to men!)

4. Weave ye the wreaths unfading,
  The fir tree and the pine;
Green from the snows of winter,
  To deck the holy shrine;
Bring ye the happy children!
  For this is Christmas morn;
Jesus, the sinless infant,
  Jesus the Lord, is born.
    (CHORUS.
  Glory to God!—to God again!
  Peace, peace on earth, good will to men!)
                    Washburne.

---

## THE EPIPHANY.

*The Manifestation of Christ to the Gentiles.*

Isaiah lx. 3. Matt. ii. 11.

### 42.         T. 79.

The wise men from the East ador'd
The infant Jesus as their Lord,
Brought gifts to Him their King:
Jesus, grant us Thy light, that we
The way may find, and unto Thee,
Our hearts, our all, a tribute bring.
                    Ancient.

## THE EPIPHANY.

C. M. [Antioch.] **43.** T. 14.

Joy to the world, the Lord is come;
  Let earth receive her King;
Let every heart prepare Him room,
  And heaven and nature sing.

2. Joy to the earth, the Saviour reigns;
  Let men their songs employ;
While fields and floods, rocks, hills, and plains
  Repeat the sounding joy.

3. No more let sin and sorrow grow,
  Nor thorns infest the ground;
He comes to make His blessings flow
  Far as the curse is found.

4. He rules the world with truth and grace,
  And makes the nations prove
The glories of His righteousness,
  And wonders of His love.

*Watts.*

7s. & 6s. **44.** T. 151.

Hail to the Lord's Anointed!
  Great David's greater Son!
Hail, in the time appointed,
  His reign on earth begun!
He comes to break oppression,
  To set the captive free,
To take away transgression,
  And rule in equity.

2. He shall come down like showers
  Upon the fruitful earth:
And joy and hope, like flowers,
  Spring in His path to birth;
Before Him, on the mountains,
  Shall peace, the herald, go:

## THE EPIPHANY.

 And righteousness, in fountains,
  From hill to valley flow.

3. Arabia's desert-ranger
  To Him shall bow the knee;
The Ethiopian stranger
  His glory come to see:
With offerings of devotion
  Ships from the isles shall meet,
To pour the wealth of ocean
  In tribute at His feet.

4. Kings shall fall down before Him,
  And gold and incense bring;
All nations shall adore Him,
  His praise all people sing:
For He shall have dominion
  O'er river, sea, and shore,
Far as the eagle's pinion,
  Or dove's light wing can soar.

5. For Him shall prayer unceasing
  And daily vows ascend;
His kingdom still increasing,—
  A kingdom without end:
The mountain-dew shall nourish
  A seed in weakness sown,
Whose fruit shall spread and flourish,
  And shake like Lebanon.

6. O'er every foe victorious,
  He on His throne shall rest;
From age to age more glorious,
  All blessing and all blest:
The tide of time shall never
  His covenant remove:
His name shall stand for ever,
  His great, best name of love.

       Montgomery.

## THE EPIPHANY.

C. M. [Coronation.]     **45.**     T. 14.

All hail the power of Jesus' name!
  Let angels prostrate fall:
Bring forth the royal diadem,
  And crown Him Lord of all.

2. Crown Him, ye martyrs of our God,
  Who from His altar call;
Praise Him who shed for you His blood
  And crown Him Lord of all.

3. Ye chosen seed of Israel's race,
  Ye ransom'd from the fall,
Hail Him who saves you by His grace,
  And crown Him Lord of all.

4. Sinners, whose love can ne'er forget
  The wormwood and the gall,
Go, spread your trophies at His feet,
  And crown Him Lord of all.

5. Let every kindred, every tribe,
  On this terrestrial ball,
To Him all majesty ascribe,
  And crown Him Lord of all.

                                      Edw. Perronet.

---

## CHRIST'S LIFE AND EXAMPLE.

Mark vii. 37.    John xiv. 6.    Matt. iv. 19.

C. M.     **46.**     T. 14

My God a man, a man indeed,
  An infant weak and poor:
Born for a sinful race to bleed,
  Salvation to procure!

## CHRIST'S LIFE AND EXAMPLE.

2. To comfort men was His delight,
    To help them in distress;
He ready was by day and night
    To pardon, heal, and bless.

3. Oft was He hungry, spent, and sad,
    In His own world a guest,
And of His own no place He had,
    His weary head to rest.

4. Ah, might my heart a mirror be,
    Reflecting Jesus' grace,
That all who my behavior see,
    May some resemblance trace.

5. Grant me that meek and lowly mind,
    Thou hast on earth display'd,
Which in Thy holy life I find,
    My Pattern, Lord and Head.

*Swertner.*

## 47.

7s.  T. 11.

See, my soul, God ever blest
In the flesh made manifest;
Human nature He assumes,
He to ransom sinners comes.

2. He fulfill'd all righteousness,
Standing in the sinner's place:
From the manger to the cross
All He did, He did for us:—

3. All our woes He did retrieve;
He expir'd that we might live;
By His stripes our wounds are heal'd,
By His blood our pardon's seal'd.

4. Lord, conform us to Thy death,
Raise us to new life by faith;
Through Thy resurrection's power,
May we praise Thee evermore.

CHRIST'S LIFE AND EXAMPLE.

5. In Thy righteousness array'd
Let us triumph and be glad;
Let us walk with Thee in white,
Let us see Thy face in light.

Hammond.

L. M.   **48.**   T. 22.

My dear Redeemer, and my Lord,
I read my duty in Thy word;
But in Thy life the law appears
Drawn out in living characters.

2. Such was Thy truth, and such Thy zeal,
Such deference to Thy Father's will,
Such love, and meekness so divine,
I would transcribe and make them mine.

3. Cold mountains and the midnight air
Witness'd the fervor of Thy pray'r:
The desert Thy temptations knew,
Thy conflict and Thy victory too.

4. Be Thou my pattern; let me bear
More of Thy gracious image here;
And at Thy right hand me confess,
Clad in Thy robe of righteousness.

Watts.

C. M.   **49.**   T. 14.

O Son of God and man, receive
This humble work of mine;
Worth to my meanest labor give,
By blessing it with Thine.

2. Servant of all, to toil for man
Thou didst not, Lord, refuse;
Thy majesty did not disdain
To be employ'd for us.

CHRIST'S LIFE AND EXAMPLE.

3. In all I think, or speak, or do,
  Let me show forth Thy praise;
Thy bright example still pursue
  Through all my future days.

## 50.    T. 79.

May Jesus Christ, the spotless Lamb,
Who to the temple humbly came
  The legal rights to pay,
Subdue our proud and stubborn will,
That we His precepts may fulfill,
  Whate'er rebellious nature say.

*Ancient.*

C. M.

## 51.    T. 14.

In duties and in sufferings too
  My Lord I fain would trace;
As Thou hast done, so would I do,
  Depending on Thy grace.

2. Inflam'd with zeal, 'twas Thy delight,
  To do Thy father's will;
May the same zeal my soul excite,
  Thy precepts to fulfill.

3. Meekness, humility, and love,
  Through all Thy conduct shine;
O may my whole deportment prove,
  A copy, Lord, of Thine.

*Beddome.*

S. M.

## 52.    T. 582.

Teach me, my God and King,
  In all things Thee to view;
And what I do in anything,
  For Thee alone to do:—

2. To scorn the senses' sway,
   While still to Thee I tend:
In all I do be Thou the way,
   In all be Thou the end.

3. All may of Thee partake;
   Nothing so small can be
But draws, when acted for Thy sake,
   Greatness and worth from Thee.

4. If done to obey Thy laws,
   Ev'n servile labors shine;
Hallow'd is toil; if this the cause,
   The meanest work divine.

Herbert.

7s. & 6s.

## 53.

T. 151.

The author of salvation,
   The Saviour, meek and mild,
Once took a lowly station,—
   Became a little child;
In infancy a stranger,
   How mean was His abode!
His cradle was a manger,
   Himself the Son of God.

2. His earthly parents found Him
   Submissive day by day;
So meek to all around Him,
   So ready to obey;
No stain of sin or folly
   Could ever cloud His brow
His heart, so pure and holy,
   With love would ever glow.

3. And when His foes assailed Him
   He sought but to forgive;
When to the cross they nailed Him,
   He died that they might live.

## CHRIST'S LIFE AND EXAMPLE.

This bright example shows us
  What duties to fulfill;
Oh, let it now arouse us
  To learn and do His will.

C. M.

## 54.

T. 14.

When for some little insult given,
  My angry passions rise,
I'll think how Jesus came from heaven,
  And bore His injuries.

2. He was insulted every day,
  Though all His words were kind;
But nothing men could do or say,
  Disturbed His heavenly mind,

3. Not all the wicked scoffs He heard
  Against the truths He taught,
Excited one reviling word,
  Or one revengeful thought.

4. And when upon the cross He bled,
  With all His foes in view,
"Father, forgive their sin," He said,
  "They know not what they do."

5. Dear Jesus, may I learn of Thee
  My temper to amend;
But speak the pardoning word for me,
  Whenever I offend.

7s.

## 55.

T. 11.

Lamb of God, I look to Thee,
Thou shalt my example be;
When Thou wast a little child,
Thou wast gentle, meek, and mild.

## CHRIST'S LIFE AND EXAMPLE.

2. Due obedience Thou didst show;
O make me obedient too.
Thou wast merciful and kind;
Grant me, Lord, Thy loving mind.

3. Let me above all fulfill
God my heavenly Father's will,
Never His good Spirit grieve,
Only to His glory live.

4. Loving Jesus, holy Lamb,
In Thy hands secure I am;
Fix Thy temple in my heart,
Never from Thy child depart.

5. Teach me to show forth Thy praise,
Love and serve thee all my days;
O might all around me see
Christ, the holy child, in me.

7s. & 6s.
## 56.

I want to be like Jesus,
  So lowly and so meek;
For no one marked an angry word,
  That ever heard Him speak.

2. I want to be like Jesus,
  So frequently in prayer;
Alone upon the mountain top,
  He met His Father there.

3. I want to be like Jesus,
  For never do I find
That He, though persecuted, was
  To any one unkind.

4. I want to be like Jesus,
  Engaged in doing good,
So that of me it may be said,
  "She hath done what she could."

## PALM SUNDAY.

5. Alas! I'm not like Jesus,
   As any one may see;
Oh, gentle Saviour, send Thy grace
   And make me like to Thee.

---

*Palm Sunday.*
John xii. 15.

C. M.  **57.**  T. 14.

Hosanna! raise the pealing hymn
   To David's Son and Lord;
With Cherubim and Seraphim
   Exalt the Incarnate Word.

2. Hosanna! Lord, our feeble tongue,
   No lofty strains can raise:
But Thou wilt not despise the young,
   Who meekly chant Thy praise.

3. Hosanna! Sovereign, Prophet, Priest,
   How vast Thy gifts, how free!
Thy Blood, our life; Thy Word, our feast;
   Thy Name, our only plea.

4. Hosanna! Master, lo! we bring
   Our offerings to Thy Throne;
Not gold, nor myrrh, nor mortal thing,
   But hearts to be Thine own.

5. Hosanna! once Thy gracious ear
   Approved a lisping throng;
Be gracious still, and deign to hear
   Our poor but grateful song.

6. O Saviour, if, redeemed by Thee,
   Thy temple we behold,
Hosannas through eternity
   We'll sing to harps of gold.

## THE SUFFERINGS OF CHRIST.

C. M.        **58.**        T. 14.

When Jesus into Salem rode,
　The children sang around;
For joy they pluck'd the palms, and strew'd
　Their garments on the ground.

2. Hosanna, our glad voices raise,
　Hosanna to our King;
Should we forget our Saviour's praise,
　The stones themselves would sing.

3. For we have learn'd to love His name;
　That name, divinely sweet,
May every pulse through life proclaim,
　And our last breath repeat.

　　　　　　　　　　　Montgomery.

---

### THE SUFFERINGS OF CHRIST.

Is. liii. 4, 5.　1 Pet. iii. 18.　Rev. i. 5, 6.

8s. & 7s. Double.    **59.**    T. 167.

Great High-priest, we view Thee stooping
With our names upon Thy breast,
In the garden, groaning, drooping,
To the ground with horrors press'd:
Angels saw, struck with amazement,
Their Creator suffer thus;
We are fill'd with deep abasement,
Since we know 'twas done for us.

2. Jesus, to the garden lead us,
To behold Thy bloody sweat;
Tho' Thou from the curse hast freed us,
May we ne'er the cost forget:

## THE SUFFERINGS OF CHRIST.

Be Thy groans and cries rehearsed
By Thy Spirit in our ears,
Till we, viewing whom we pierced,
Melt in penitential tears.

*Hart.*

## 60.

7s.   T. 581.

Go to dark Gethsemane,
Ye that feel the tempter's power,
Your Redeemer's conflict see,
Watch with Him one bitter hour.
Turn not from His griefs away,
Learn of Jesus Christ to pray.

2. Follow to the judgment-hall,
View the Lord of life arraign'd.
O the wormwood and the gall!
O the pangs His soul sustain'd!
Shun not suffering, shame or loss;
Learn of Him to bear the cross.

3. Calvary's mournful mountain climb,
There, adoring at His feet,
Mark that miracle of time,
God's own sacrifice complete.
"It is finish'd!" hear Him cry;
Learn of Jesus Christ to die.

4. Early hasten to the tomb,
Where they laid His breathless clay.
All is solitude and gloom,
Who hath taken Him away?
Christ is ris'n—He meets our eyes;
Saviour, teach us so to rise.

*Montgomery.*

## THE SUFFERINGS OF CHRIST.

C. M. **61.** T. 14

Alas! and did my Saviour bleed?
   And did my Sovereign die?
Would He devote His sacred head
   For such a worm as I?

2. Was it for crimes that I had done,
   He groan'd upon the tree?
Amazing pity! grace unknown!
   And love beyond degree!

3. Well might the sun in darkness hide
   And shut His glories in,
When the almighty Maker died,
   An offering for my sin.

4. Thus might I hide my blushing face,
   While Jesus' cross appears;
Dissolve, my heart, in thankfulness,
   And melt my eyes in tears.

5. But drops of grief can ne'er repay
   The debt of love I owe;
Here, Lord, I give myself away;
   'Tis all that I can do.

                                  Watts.

L. M. Double. **62.** T. 166.

When I survey the wondrous cross
On which the Prince of Glory died,
My richest gain I count but loss,
And pour contempt on all my pride.
Forbid it, Lord, that I should boast
In aught beside my ransom-price;
All the vain things which charm'd me most,
For Christ I freely sacrifice.

## THE SUFFERINGS OF CHRIST.

2. See from His head, His hands, His feet,
Sorrow and love flow mingled down;
Did e'er such love and sorrow meet,
Or thorns compose so rich a crown?
Were the whole realm of nature mine,
That were a present far too small;
Love so amazing, so divine,
Demands my soul, my life, my all.

Watts.

## 63.

C. M.     T. 14.

There is a fountain fill'd with blood,
  Drawn from Immanuel's veins;
And sinners plung'd beneath that flood,
  Lose all their guilty stains.

2. The dying thief rejoic'd to see
  That fountain in his day;
And there have I, as vile as he,
  Wash'd all my sins away.

3. E'er since by faith I saw the stream,
  Thy flowing wounds supply,
Redeeming love has been my theme,
  And shall be till I die.

4. Then in a nobler, sweeter song
  I'll sing Thy power to save,
When this poor lisping, stammering tongue
  Lies silent in the grave.

Cowper.

## 64.

8s. & 7s.     T. 16.

Sweet the moments, rich in blessing,
Which before the cross I spend;
Life and health and peace possessing,
From the sinner's dying Friend.

## THE SUFFERINGS OF CHRIST.

2. Here I'll sit, for ever viewing
Mercy's streams in streams of blood:
Precious drops, my soul bedewing,
Plead and claim my peace with God.

3. Truly blessed is this station,
Low before His cross to lie;
While I see divine compassion
Floating in His languid eye.

4. Here it is I find my heaven,
While upon the cross I gaze;
Love I much? I've much forgiven,
I'm a miracle of grace.

5. Love and grief my heart dividing,
With my tears His feet I'll bathe;
Constant still in faith abiding,
Life deriving from His death.

6. May I still enjoy this feeling,
In all need to Jesus go;
Prove His wounds each day more healing,
And Himself more fully know.

Walter Shirley.

8s. & 7s. Double.  **65.**  T. 167.

Hail, Thou once despised Jesus!
  Hail, thou Galilean King!
Thou didst suffer to release us,
  Thou didst free salvation bring.
Hail, Thou agonizing Saviour,
  Bearer of our sin and shame!
By Thy merits we find favor;
  Life is given through Thy Name!

2. Paschal Lamb, by God appointed,
  All our sins on Thee were laid;
By almighty love anointed,
  Thou hast full atonement made;

Every sin may be forgiven
  Through the virtue of Thy blood;
Opened is the gate to heaven;
  Man is reconciled to God.

                              Bakewell.

## 66.                         T. 151. a.

O head so full of bruises,
  So full of pain and scorn,
Midst other sore abuses
  Mock'd with a crown of thorn;
O head, ere now surrounded
  With brightest majesty,
In death now bow'd and wounded,
  Saluted be by me!

2. I give Thee thanks unfeigned,
  O Jesus, friend in need,
For what Thy soul sustained,
  When Thou for me didst bleed.
Grant me to lean unshaken
  Upon Thy faithfulness,
Until I hence am taken,
  To see Thee face to face.

3. Lord, at my dissolution
  Do not from me depart;
Support at the conclusion
  Of life, my fainting heart;
And when I pine and languish,
  Seiz'd with death's agony,
O by Thy pain and anguish
  Set me at liberty.

4. Lord, grant me Thy protection,
  Remind me of Thy death
And glorious resurrection,
  When I resign my breath:

THE SUFFERINGS OF CHRIST.

Ah, then, though I be dying
 Midst sickness, grief, and pain,
I shall, on Thee relying,
 Eternal life obtain.

*Gerhard & Z.*

---

*The Burial of Jesus.*

8s. & 7s. Double.    **67.**    T. 167.

Lord of life! now sweetly slumber,
 With the dead awhile a guest,
After torments without number,
 Glorious is Thy hard-earn'd rest.
Lo! the dreadful conflict's ended;
 By Thy suffering Thou hast won;
Now o'er all Thy power's extended,
 E'en my heart O claim Thy own.

2. O what love is here displayed!
 See the Father's only Son
To the silent tomb conveyed;
 Ah, my soul, what hast thou done!
Yet, while I, my sins bewailing,
 Own that they His blood have spilt,
May that blood, for me prevailing,
 Wash away my sin and guilt.

7s.    **68.**    T. 11. b.

Go, my soul, go every day
To the tomb where Jesus lay;
Be with Him my members dead,
Be His sepulchre my bed.

2. Boldest foes dare never come
Near my Saviour's sacred tomb;
Evil never can molest
Those who near His body rest.

*Worthington.*

## THE RESURRECTION OF CHRIST.

*Easter.*

Romans xiv. 9.

### 69.

S. M.   T. 595.

Christians, dismiss your fear;
  Let hope and joy succeed;
The joyful news with gladness hear,
  "The Lord is ris'n indeed."
The promise is fulfill'd
  In Christ our only Head;
Justice with mercy's reconcil'd;
  He lives who once was dead.

2. The Lord is ris'n again,
  Who on the cross did bleed:
He lives to die no more, Amen!
  The Lord is ris'n indeed.
He truly tasted death
  For wretched fallen man;
In bitter pangs resign'd His breath;
  But now is ris'n again.

### 70.

T. 185.

Hail, all hail, victorious Lord and Saviour!
Thou hast burst the bonds of death.
Grant us, as to Mary, that great favor
To embrace Thy feet in faith.
Thou hast in our stead the curse endured,
And for us eternal life procured;
Joyful, we with one accord
Hail Thee as our risen Lord.

2. O Thou matchless source of consolation,
Scarce Thy resting moments end,

ASCENSION AND GLORY OF CHRIST.

When a heart-enlivening salutation
To Thy followers Thou dost send:
We would share Thy dear disciples' feeling
When before their risen Master kneeling:
Thus shall we with all our heart
Witness what a friend Thou art.

*Louisa v. Hayn.*

L. M.
## 71.
T. 22.

I know that my Redeemer lives:
What joy this sweet assurance gives!
He lives, He lives, who once was dead,
He lives, my ever-living Head.

2. He lives, to bless me with His love,
He lives, to plead for me above,
He lives, my hungry soul to feed,
He lives, to help in time of need.

3. He lives, to silence all my fears,
He lives, to stop and wipe my tears,
He lives, to calm my troubled heart,
He lives, all blessings to impart.

4. He lives, all glory to His name!
He lives, my Jesus, still the same;
Oh, the sweet joy this sentence gives:
I know that my Redeemer lives!

*C. Wesley.*

---

## ASCENSION AND GLORY OF CHRIST.

1 Peter iii. 22.

C. M.
## 72.
T. 14.

The Lord ascendeth up on high,
 Deck'd with resplendent wounds;
While shouts of victory rend the sky,
 And heaven with joy resounds.

ASCENSION AND GLORY OF CHRIST.

2. Eternal gates their leaves unfold,
   Receive the conquering King,
The angels strike their harps of gold,
   And saints triumphant sing.

3. Sinners, rejoice, He died for you,
   For you prepares a place,
His Spirit sends, you to endow
   With every gift and grace.

4. His blood, which did for you atone,
   For your salvation pleads;
And, seated on His Father's throne,
   He reigns and intercedes.

*Hart.*

## 73.

S. M.  T. 595.

Jesus who died, is now
   Seated upon His throne:
The angels who before Him bow,
   His just dominion own.

2. The unworthiest of His friends
   Upon His heart He bears;
He ever to their cause attends,
   For them a place prepares.

3. Blest Saviour, condescend
   My advocate to be;
I could not have a better friend
   To plead with God for me.

*Watts.*

## 74.

L. M.  T 22.

Where high the heavenly temple stands,
The house of God not made with hands,
A great High-Priest our nature wears,
The guardian of mankind appears.

6

## ASCENSION AND GLORY OF CHRIST.

2. Though now ascended up on high,
He bends to earth a brother's eye;
Partaker of the human name,
He knows the frailty of our frame.

3. Our fellow-sufferer yet retains
A fellow-feeling of our pains;
And still remembers, in the skies,
His tears, His agonies, and cries.

4. In every pang that rends the heart,
The man of sorrows bears a part;
He sympathizes with our grief,
And to the sufferer sends relief.

5. With boldness, therefore, at the throne
Let us make all our sorrow known;
And ask the aid of heavenly power,
To help us in the evil hour.

*Logan.*

8s. & 7s. Double. **75.** T. 167.

Jesus, hail! enthroned in glory,
  There forever to abide!
All the heavenly hosts adore Thee,
  Seated at Thy Father's side:
There for sinners Thou art pleading;
  There Thou dost our place prepare,
Ever for us interceding,
  Till in glory Thou appear.

2. Worship, honor, power and blessing,
  Thou art worthy to receive;
Loudest praises, without ceasing,
  Meet it is for us to give:
Help, ye bright, angelic spirits,
  Bring your sweetest, noblest lays,
Help to sing our Saviour's merits,
  Help to chant Immanuel's praise.

*Bakewell.*

## ASCENSION AND GLORY OF CHRIST.

C. M.  **76.**  T. 14.

O the delights, the heavenly joys,
The glories of the place,
Where Jesus sheds the brightest beams
Of His o'erflowing grace.

2. Sweet majesty and awful love
Sit smiling on His brow,
And all the glorious ranks above,
At humble distance bow.

3. Princes to His imperial name
Bend their bright sceptres down;
Dominions, thrones and powers rejoice
To see Him wear the crown.

4. Upon that dear majestic head,
That cruel thorns did wound,
See what immortal glories shine
And circle it around.

5. This is the Man, the exalted Man,
Whom we unseen adore;
But when our eyes shall see His face,
Our hearts shall love Him more.

Watts.

C. M. Double.  **77.**  T. 590.

We sing Thy praise exalted Lamb,
Who sit'st upon the throne:
Ten thousand blessings to Thy name
Who worthy art alone.
Thy sacred, bruised body bore
Our sins upon the tree:
And now Thou livest evermore;
O may we live to Thee.

2. Poor sinners, sing the Lamb that died:
(What theme can sound so sweet?)

ASCENSION AND GLORY OF CHRIST.

His drooping head, His streaming side,
His pierced hands and feet;
With all that scene of suffering love,
Which faith presents to view:
For now He reigns and lives above,
Yea, lives and reigns for you.

L. M.

## 78.

T. 22.

Jesus shall reign where'er the sun
Doth his successive journeys run:
His kingdom stretch from shore to shore,
Till moons shall wax and wane no more.

2. For Him shall endless prayer be made,
And praises throng to crown His head;
His name like sweet perfume shall rise
With every morning sacrifice.

3. People and realms of every tongue
Dwell on His love with sweetest song,
And infant voices shall proclaim
Their early blessing on His name.

4. Blessings abound where'er he reigns,
The prisoner leaps to lose His chains,
The weary find eternal rest,
And all the sons of want are blest.

5. Let every creature rise and bring
Peculiar honors to our King:
Angels descend with songs again,
And earth repeat the loud Amen.

Watts.

L. M.

## 79.

T. 22.

From all that dwell below the skies
Let the Creator's praise arise;
Let the Redeemer's name be sung
Through every land, by every tongue.

2. Eternal are Thy mercies, Lord;
Eternal truth attends Thy word:
Thy praise shall sound from shore to shore,
Till suns shall rise and set no more.
Watts.

## THE HOLY SPIRIT.

*Whitsunday.*

### Acts ii. 33.

# 80.  T. 22.

O Comforter, God Holy Ghost,
Thou heavenly gifts on us bestow'st;
The pledge of our salvation art,
And bear'st Thy witness in our heart.

2. The sheep of Jesus which were lost
Thou callest, teaching them to trust
For help, forgiveness, peace, and grace
In Him, the Lord our righteousness.

3. Thy gladd'ning oil Thou dost impart
To every poor and contrite heart,
Which Jesus as the Saviour knows,
From whom alone salvation flows.

4. The feeble souls Thou dost sustain,
Anointest all the witness train,
Keepest believers in the faith,
And art their guide in life and death.

5. Who can Thy operations trace,
The kindness, patience, truth and grace,
Thou showest to Christ's family,
Who living temples are to Thee.
Bohemian Brethren.

## THE HOLY SPIRIT.

### 81.

M.    T. 14.

Come, Holy Spirit, on us breathe
With all Thy quickening powers;
Kindle our love, confirm our faith,
Warm these cold hearts of ours.

2. Assure my conscience of her part
In the Redeemer's blood;
And bear Thy witness in my heart,
That I am born of God.

3. Thou art the earnest of His love,
The pledge of joys to come:
O lead us, that we may above
Obtain our lasting home.

*Watts.*

### 82.

L. M.    T. 22.

To Thee, God Holy Ghost, we pray,
Who lead'st us in the gospel-way,
Those precious gifts on us bestow,
Which from our Saviour's merits flow.

2. Thou heavenly Teacher, Thee we praise
For Thy instruction, power, and grace,
To love the Father, who doth own
Us as His children in the Son.

3. Most gracious Comforter, we pray,
O lead us further every day;
Thy unction to us all impart,
Preserve and sanctify each heart.

4. Till we in heaven shall take our seat,
Instruct us often to repeat,
"Abba, our Father," and to be
With Christ in union constantly.

*Zinzendorf.*

## THE HOLY SPIRIT.

C M.   **83.**   T. 1L

Come, Holy Spirit, heavenly Dove,
   With all Thy quickening powers;
Kindle a flame of sacred love
   In these cold hearts of ours.

2. In vain we tune our formal songs;
   In vain we strive to rise;
Hosannas languish on our tongues,
   And our devotion dies.

3. Dear Lord, and shall we ever live
   At this poor, dying rate,
Our love so faint, so cold to Thee,
   And Thine to us so great?

4. Come, Holy Spirit, heavenly Dove,
   With all Thy quickening powers,
Come, shed abroad a Saviour's love,
   And that shall kindle ours.

*Watts.*

L. M.   **84.**   T. 22

O Spirit of the living God,
   In all Thy plenitude of grace,
Where'er the foot of man hath trod,
   Descend on our apostate race.

2. Give tongues of fire, and hearts of love,
   To preach the reconciling word:
Give power and unction from above,
   Where'er the joyful sound is heard.

3. Be darkness, at Thy coming, light;
   Confusion—order, in Thy path;
Souls without strength, inspire with might:
   Bid mercy triumph over wrath.

## THE HOLY TRINITY.

4. Baptize the nations; far and nigh
   The triumphs of the cross record;
The name of Jesus glorify,
   Till every kindred call Him Lord.

Montgomery.

---

### THE HOLY TRINITY.

#### 1 John v. 7.

## 85. T. 68.

Holy Trinity,
  We confess with joy,
That our life and whole salvation
Flow from God's blest incarnation,
  And His death for us
  On the shameful cross.

2. Had we angels' tongues
   With seraphic songs,
Bowing hearts and knees before Thee,
Triune God, we would adore Thee,
   In the highest strain,
   For the Lamb once slain.

Nyberg.

## 86. T. 39.

11s.

O Father of mercy, be ever ador'd;
Thy love was displayed in sending our Lord,
To ransom and bless us: Thy goodness we praise
For sending in Jesus salvation by grace.

2. Most merciful Saviour, who deignedst to die
Our curse to remove, and our pardon to buy,
Accept our thanksgiving, almighty to save,
Who openest heaven to all that believe.

INVITATION AND WARNING. 89

3. O Spirit of wisdom, of love, and of power,
We prove Thy blest influence, Thy grace we adore;
Whose inward revealing applies our Lord's blood,
Attesting and sealing us children of God.

C. Wesley.

C. M. **87.** T. 14.

Our heavenly Father, source of love,
  To Thee our hearts we raise:
Thy all-sustaining power we prove,
  And gladly sing Thy praise.

2. Lord Jesus, Thine we wish to be,
  Our sacrifice receive:
Made, and preserv'd, and sav'd by Thee,
  To Thee ourselves we give.

3. Come, Holy Ghost, the Saviour's love
  Shed in our hearts abroad:
So shall we ever live, and move,
  And be with Christ in God.

4. Honor to the Almighty Three,
  And everlasting One,
All glory to the Father be,
  The Spirit, and the Son.

---

## CHRISTIAN LIFE.—I. INVITATION AND WARNING.

Rev xxii. 17.

8s. 7s. & 4s. **88.** T. 585.

Come, ye sinners, poor and needy,
  Weak and wounded, sick and sore,
Jesus ready stands to save you,

## INVITATION AND WARNING.

    Full of pity, love, and power:
      He is able, :||:
He is willing; doubt no more.

2. Ho, ye needy, come and welcome:
    God's free bounty glorify:
True belief, and true repentance,
    Every grace that brings us nigh,
      Without money, :||:
Come to Jesus Christ and buy.

3. Come, ye weary, heavy-laden,
    Lost and ruin'd by the fall:
If ye tarry till ye're better,
    Ye will never come at all:
      Not the righteous, :||:
Sinners Jesus came to call.

4. Let not conscience make you linger,
    Nor of fitness fondly dream;
All the fitness He requireth,
    Is to feel your need of Him:
      This He gives you; :||:
'Tis the Spirit's glimmering beam.

5. Agonizing in the garden,
    Lo your Maker prostrate lies:
On the bloody tree behold Him,
    Hear Him cry, before He dies,
      "It is finished;" :||:
Sinners, will not this suffice?

6. Lo, the incarnate God ascended,
    Pleads the merit of His blood:
Venture on Him, venture freely,
    Let no other trust intrude;
      None but Jesus :||:
Can do helpless sinners good.

7. Saints and angels, join'd in concert,
    Sing the praises of the Lamb;

## INVITATION AND WARNING.

While the blissful seats of heaven
  Sweetly echo with His name:
    Hallelujah, :||:
Sinners here may sing the same.

*Cennick.*

L. M.

## 89.

T. 22.

Behold a Stranger at the door!
He gently knocks, has knock'd before;
Has waited long—is waiting still;
You treat no other friend so ill.

2. Oh! lovely attitude—He stands
With melting heart and loaded hands:
Oh! matchless kindness—and He shows
This matchless kindness to His foes.

3. But will He prove a friend indeed?
He will,—the very friend you need;
The friend of sinners—yes, 'tis He,
With garments dyed on Calvary!

4. Rise, touch'd with gratitude divine;
Turn out His enemy and thine,
That soul-destroying monster, sin,
And let the heavenly Stranger in.

5. Admit Him, ere His anger burn—
His feet departed, ne'er return;
Admit Him, or the hour's at hand
You'll at His door rejected stand.

*Gregg.*

7s.

## 90.

T. 205 or 11.

Sinners, turn; why will ye die?
God, your Maker, asks you why?
God, who did your being give,
Made you with Himself to live.

INVITATION AND WARNING.

He the fatal cause demands,
Asks the work of His own hands,—
Why, ye thankless creatures, why
Will ye cross His love, and die?

2. Sinners, turn; why will ye die?
God, your Saviour, asks you why;
He, who did your souls retrieve,
Died Himself, that you might live.
Will ye let Him die in vain?
Crucify your Lord again?
Why, ye ransom'd sinners, why
Will ye slight His grace, and die?

3. Sinners, turn; why will ye die?
God, the Spirit, asks you why?
He, who all your lives hath strove,
Urged you to embrace His love.
Will ye not His grace receive?
Will ye still refuse to live?
Oh, ye dying sinners, why,
Why will ye forever die?

C. Wesley.

## 91.

C. M.  T. 14.

See, the kind Shepherd, Jesus, stands,
  And calls His sheep by name;
Gathers the feeble in His arms,
  And feeds each tender Lamb.

2. He'll lead us to the heavenly streams
  Where living waters flow;
And guide us to the fruitful fields
  Where trees of knowledge grow.

3. When, wand'ring from the fold, we leave
  The straight and narrow way,
Our faithful Shepherd still is near
  To guide us when we stray.

INVITATION AND WARNING.

4. The feeblest lamb amidst the flock
Shall be the Shepherd's care;
While folded in our Saviour's arms,
We're safe from every snare.

L. M.
## 92.
T 22. a.

Just as Thou art,—without one trace
Of love, or joy, or inward grace,
Or meetness for the heavenly place,—
O guilty sinner, come! O come!

2. Thy sins I bore on Calvary's tree;
The stripes thy due were laid on me,
That peace and pardon might be free,—
O wretched sinner, come! O come!

3. Come, leave thy burden at the cross;
Count all thy gains but empty dross;
My grace repays all earthly loss,—
O needy sinner, come! O come!

4. Come, hither bring thy boding fears,
Thy aching heart, thy bursting tears;
'Tis mercy's voice salutes thine ears,—
O trembling sinner, come! O come!

5. The Spirit and the bride say, "Come!"
Rejoicing saints re-echo, "Come!"
Who faints, who thirsts, who will, may come:
Thy Saviour bids thee come! O come!

P. M.*
## 93.

We're traveling home to heaven above,
  Will you go? :||:
To sing the Saviour's dying love,
  Will you go? :||:
Millions have reached that blest abode,

\* Songs of Devotion, p. 246.

Anointed kings and priests to God,
And millions more are on the road,
    Will you go? :||:

2. We're going to see the bleeding Lamb,
    Will you go? :||:
In rapturous strains to praise His name,
    Will you go? :||:
The crown of life we there shall wear,
The conqueror's palms our hands shall bear,
And all the joys of heaven we'll share,
    Will you go? :||:

3. Ye weary, heavy-laden, come,
    Will you go? :||:
In the blest house there still is room,
    Will you go? :||:
The Lord is waiting to receive;
If thou wilt on Him now believe,
He'll give thy troubled conscience ease,
    Come, believe. :||:

4. The way to heaven is straight and plain,
    Will you go? :||:
Repent, believe, be born again,
    Will you go? :||:
The Saviour cries aloud to thee,
"Take up thy cross and follow me,
And thou shalt my salvation see,
    Come to me." :||:

8s. 7s. & 4s. **94.** T. 585.

Children, hear the melting story
    Of the Lamb that once was slain;
'Tis the Lord of life and glory;
    Shall He plead with you in vain?
        Oh receive Him, :||:
    And salvation now obtain.

2. Yield no more to sin and folly,
   So displeasing in His sight;
Jesus loves the pure and holy,
   They alone are His delight;
      Seek His favor, :‖:
   And your hearts to Him unite.

3. All your sins to Him confessing
   Who is ready to forgive,
Seek the Saviour's richest blessing,
   On His precious name believe;
      He is waiting: :‖:
   Will you not His grace receive?

## II. REPENTANCE.

Ps. li. 17. Acts iii. 19.

### 95.

S. M.       T. 582.

O Lord, how vile am I,
   Unholy and unclean!
How can I venture to draw nigh
   With such a load of sin?
And must I then indeed
   Sink in despair and die?
Fain would I hope that Thou didst bleed
   For such a wretch as I.

2. That blood which Thou hast spilt,
     That grace which is Thine own,
   Can cleanse the vilest sinner's guilt,
     And soften hearts of stone:
   Low at Thy feet I bow,
     O pity and forgive:
   Here will I lie, and wait till Thou
     Shalt bid me rise and live.

*Newton.*

## REPENTANCE.

L. M.   **96.**   T. 22.

Show pity, Lord, O Lord forgive;
Let a repenting sinner live,
Are not Thy mercies large and free?
May not a sinner trust in Thee?

2. My crimes are great, but don't surpass
The power and glory of Thy grace;
Great God, Thy nature hath no bound,—
So let Thy pard'ning love be found.

3. Oh, wash my soul from every sin,
And make my guilty conscience clean;
Here on my heart the burden lies,
And past offences pain my eyes.

4. My lips with shame my sins confess
Against Thy law, against Thy grace;
Lord, should Thy judgments grow severe,
I am condemn'd, but Thou art clear.

5. Should sudden vengeance seize my breath,
I must pronounce Thee just, in death;
And if my soul were sent to hell,
Thy righteous law approves it well.

6. Yet save a trembling sinner, Lord,
Whose hope, still hov'ring round Thy word,
Would light on some sweet promise there—
Some sure support against despair.

*Watts.*

7s.   **97.**   T. 581 or 83.

Saviour of Thy chosen race,
　View me from Thy heavenly throne;
Give the sweet relenting grace,
　Soften Thou this heart of stone:
Stone to flesh, O God, convert,
Cast a look, and break my heart.

2. By Thy Spirit me reprove,
   All my inmost sins reveal;
Sins against Thy light and love
   Let me see, and let me feel;
Sins, that crucified my God,
Sins, for which He shed His blood.

3. Jesus, seek Thy wandering sheep,
   Make me restless to return:
Bid me on Thee look and weep,
   Bitterly as Peter mourn:
Till I can, by grace restor'd,
Say, "Thou know'st I love Thee, Lord."

4. Might I in Thy sight appear
   As the publican distress'd;
Stand, not daring to draw near,
   Smite on my unworthy breast,
Utter the poor sinner's plea,
"God, be merciful to me."

5. Ah, remember me for good,
   Passing thro' this mortal vale;
Show me Thy atoning blood,
   When my strength and courage fail:
Let me oft in spirit see
Jesus, crucified for me.

C. I. Latrobe.

## 98.     T. 79.

Lo, on a narrow neck of land,
'Twixt two unbounded seas I stand,
Secure, insensible;
A point of time, a moment's space,
Removes me to that heavenly place,
Or ever shuts me up in hell.

2. O God, mine inmost soul convert!
And deeply on my thoughtful heart

## REPENTANCE.

Eternal things impress;
Give me to feel their solemn weight,
To tremble on the brink of fate,
And to awake to righteousness.

3. Before me place in dread array,
The pomp of that tremendous day,
When Thou with clouds shalt come,
To judge the nations at Thy bar:
And tell me, Lord, shall I be there,
To meet from Thee a joyful doom?

4. Be this my one great business here
With godly jealousy and fear,
Eternal bliss to insure;
Thine utmost counsel to fulfill,
To suffer all Thy righteous will,
And steadfast to the end endure.

5. Then, Saviour, then my soul receive,
Transported from this vale, to live
And reign with Thee above;
Where faith is sweetly lost in sight,
And hope, in full, supreme delight,
And everlasting, heavenly love.

C. Wesley.

S. M.    **99.**    T. 582.

O where shall rest be found—
  Rest for the weary soul?
'Twere vain the ocean's depths to sound,
  Or pierce to either pole.

2. The world can never give
  The rest, for which we sigh;
'Tis not the whole of life to live,
  Nor all of death to die.

3. Beyond this vale of tears
  There is a life above,

REPENTANCE.

Unmeasur'd by the flight of years—
And all that life is love.

4. There is a death, whose pang
Outlasts the fleeting breath:
Oh, what eternal horrors hang
Around the second death!

5. Thou God of truth and grace!
Teach us that death to shun;
Lest we be banished from Thy face,
For evermore undone.

*Montgomery.*

S. M.
## 100.
T. 582 or 595.

If Jesus Christ was sent,
To save us from our sin,
And kindly teach us to repent,
We should at once begin.

2. He says He loves to see
A broken-hearted one;
He loves that sinners, such as we,
Should mourn for what we've done.

3. 'Tis not enough to say,
We're sorry and repent,
Yet still go on from day to day,
Just as we always went.

4. Repentance is to leave
The sins we loved before,
And show that we in earnest grieve,
By doing so no more.

5. Lord, make us thus sincere,
To watch as well as pray;
However small, however dear,
Take all our sins away.

REPENTANCE.

6. And since the Saviour came
   To make us turn from sin,
With holy grief and humble shame
   We would at once begin.

C. M.
## 101.
T. 14 a.

O Lord, forgive a sinful child,
   Whose heart is all unclean;
How bad am I, and how defil'd,
   How prone to every sin.

2. O change my vile and stubborn heart,
   Like Thee O make me pure;
To me Thy love divine impart,
   Keep me from sin secure.

3. Self-will, that cruel enemy,
   No more I would obey;
Thy Spirit shall my teacher be,
   And guide me in Thy way.

4. O may I never speak a word
   But what I truly mean,
Nor lie to Thee, most gracious Lord,
   By whom each thought is seen.

5. I'll make Thy wondrous, dying love,
   Dear Lord, my daily song;
And joys, like theirs who sing above,
   Shall tune my infant tongue.

C. M.
## 102.
T. 14.

Approach, my soul, the mercy-seat,
   Where Jesus answers prayer:
There humbly fall before His feet,
   For none can perish there.

## REPENTANCE.

2. Thy promise is my only plea,
   With this I venture nigh;
Thou callest burden'd souls to Thee,
   And such, O Lord, am I.

3. Bow'd down beneath a load of sin,
   By Satan sorely prest;
By wars without, and fears within,
   I come to Thee for rest.

4. Be Thou my shield and hiding place!
   That, shelter'd near Thy side,
I may my fierce accuser face,
   And tell him, Thou hast died.

5. O wondrous love! to bleed and die,
   To bear the cross and shame,
That guilty sinners, such as I,
   Might plead Thy gracious name.

6. "Poor tempest-tossed soul, be still,
   My promis'd grace receive:"
'Tis Jesus speaks—I must, I will,
   I can, I do believe.

Newton.

C. M.  **103.**  T. 590 or 14.

Jesus, Thou art the sinner's friend,
   As such I look to Thee;
Now, in the fulness of Thy love,
   O Lord, remember me.
Remember Thy pure word of grace,
   Remember Calvary,
Remember all Thy dying groans,
   And then remember me.

2. Thou wondrous Advocate with God,
   I yield myself to Thee;
While Thou art sitting on Thy throne,
   Dear Lord, remember me.

I own I'm guilty, own I'm vile,
  Yet Thy salvation's free;
Then, in Thy all-abounding grace,
  Dear Lord, remember me.

3. Howe'er forsaken or distress'd,
  Howe'er oppress'd I be,
Howe'er afflicted here on earth,
  Do Thou remember me.
And when I close my eyes in death,
  And creature helps all flee,
Then, O my great Redeemer-God,
  Jesus, remember me.

*Burnham.*

## III. FAITH.

Ephesians ii. 8.  Acts x. 43.  1 John v. 4, 5.

### 104.

S. M.                                    T. 595

Faith is a precious grace,
  Where'er it is bestow'd;
It boasts of a celestial birth,
  And is the gift of God.

2. Jesus it owns as King,
  And all-atoning Priest;
It claims no merit of its own,
  But looks for all in Christ.

3. To Him it leads the soul,
  When fill'd with deep distress;
Flies to the fountain of His blood,
  And trusts His righteousness.

4. Since 'tis Thy work alone,
  And that divinely free;
Lord, send the Spirit of Thy Son
  To work this faith in me.

*Beddome.*

## FAITH.

L. M.

### 105.

T. 22.

Just as I am, without one plea,
But that Thy blood was shed for me,
And that Thou bidst me come to Thee,
O Lamb of God, I come, I come!

2. Just as I am, and waiting not
To rid my soul of one dark blot,
To Thee, whose blood can cleanse each spot,
O Lamb of God, I come, I come!

3. Just as I am, though toss'd about
With many a conflict, many a doubt,
Fightings within, and fears without,
O Lamb of God, I come, I come!

4. Just as I am, poor, wretched, blind,
Sight, riches, healing of the mind,
Yea, all I need, in Thee to find,
O Lamb of God, I come, I come!

5. Just as I am,—Thou wilt receive,
Wilt welcome, pardon, cleanse, relieve,
Because Thy promise I believe,
O Lamb of God, I come, I come!

6. Just as I am, Thy love unknown
Has broken every barrier down;
Now to be Thine, and Thine alone,
O Lamb of God, I come, I come!

*Charlotte Elliot.*

### 106.

T. 90.

O Love, Thou fathomless abyss,
My sins are swallow'd up in Thee;
Cover'd is my unrighteousness,
From condemnation now I'm free;
Since Jesus' blood, thro' earth and skies,
Mercy, free boundless mercy cries.

FAITH.

2. By faith I plunge into this sea,
Here is my hope, my joy, my rest;
Hither, when sin assails, I flee;
I look into my Saviour's breast;
Away, sad doubt and anxious fear,
Mercy is all that's written there.

3. Tho' waves and storms go o'er my head,
Tho' strength, and health, and friends be gone;
Tho' joys be wither'd all and dead,
Tho' every comfort be withdrawn:
Steadfast on this my soul relies,
Jesus, Thy mercy never dies.

4. Fix'd on this ground will I remain,
Tho' my heart fail and flesh decay;
This anchor shall my soul sustain,
When earth's foundations melt away:
Mercy's full power I then shall prove,
Lov'd with an everlasting love.

Rothe.

C. M.

## 107.

T. 14.

Hail, Alpha and Omega hail,
  Thou Author of our faith,
The Finisher of all our hopes,
  The Truth, the Life, the Path.

2. Hail, First and Last, Thou great I AM,
  In whom we live and move:
Increase our little spark of faith,
  And fill our hearts with love.

3. O let that faith which Thou hast taught,
  Be treasur'd in our breast;
The evidence of unseen joys,
  The substance of our rest.

FAITH. 105

4. Then shall we go from strength to strength,
   From grace to greater grace;
From each degree of faith to more,
   Till we behold Thy face.

Cennick.

## 108.

7s.*                         T. 581.

Rock of ages cleft for me,
Let me hide myself in Thee;
Let the water and the blood,
From Thy riven side which flow'd,
Be of sin the double cure,
Cleanse me from its guilt and power.

2. Not the labor of my hands
Can fulfil Thy law's demands:
Could my zeal no respite know,
Could my tears for ever flow,
All for sin could not atone;
Thou must save, and Thou alone.

3. Nothing in my hand I bring
Simply to Thy cross I cling,
Naked, come to Thee for dress,
Helpless, look to Thee for grace,
Vile, I to the fountain fly,—
Wash me, Saviour, or I die.

4. While I draw this fleeting breath,
When my eyes shall close in death,
When I soar to worlds unknown,
See Thee on Thy judgment-throne;
Rock of ages, cleft for me,
Let me hide myself in Thee.

Toplady.

* Songs of Devotion, p. 15.

FAITH.

L. M.

## 109.

T. 22.

The Saviour's blood and righteousness
My beauty is, my glorious dress;
Thus well array'd I need not fear,
When in His presence I appear.

2. The holy, spotless Lamb of God,
Who freely gave His life and blood
For all my numerous sins to atone,
I for my Lord and Saviour own.

3. In Him I trust for evermore,
He hath expung'd the dreadful score
Of all my guilt; this done away,
I need not fear the judgment-day.

4. Therefore my Saviour's blood and death
Is here the substance of my faith:
And shall remain, when I'm call'd hence,
My only hope and confidence.

*Zinzendorf.*

C. M.

## 110.

T. 14.

When I can read my title clear,
   To mansions in the skies,
I'll bid farewell to every fear,
   And wipe my weeping eyes.

2. Should earth against my soul engage,
   And fiery darts be hurled,
Then I can smile at Satan's rage,
   And face a frowning world.

3. Let cares like a wild deluge come,
   Let storms of sorrow fall,
So I but safely reach my home,
   My God, my heaven, my all.

FAITH. 107

4. There I shall bathe my weary soul
   In seas of heavenly rest,
And not a wave of trouble roll
   Across my peaceful breast.

Watts.

## 111.

S. M.   T. 582.

Not all the blood of beasts,
   On Jewish altars slain,
Could give the guilty conscience peace,
   Or wash away the stain.

2. Christ, the true paschal Lamb,
   Takes all our sins away;
A sacrifice of nobler name,
   And richer blood than they.

3. My faith would lay the hand
   On that dear head of thine,
While like a penitent I stand,
   And there confess my sin.

4. Lord, I look back to see
   The burden Thou didst bear,
When hanging on the shameful tree;
   And know my guilt was there.

5. Believing, we rejoice,
   Our curse He did remove;
We bless the Lamb with cheerful voice,
   And sing His bleeding love.

Watts.

## 112.

7s. & 6s.   T. 151.

How lost was my condition,
   Till Jesus made me whole;
There is but one physician
   Can cure the sin-sick soul:

FAITH.

Nigh unto death He found me,
  And snatch'd me from the grave;
To tell to all around me,
  His wondrous power to save.

2. A dying, risen Jesus,
    Seen by the eye of faith,
  At once from anguish frees us,
    And saves the soul from death;
  Come then to this physician,
    His help He'll freely give,
  He makes no hard condition,
    'Tis only—look and live.
                                    Newton.

S. M.          **113.**          T. 595.

I hear the words of love,
  I gaze upon the blood,
I see the mighty sacrifice,
  And I have peace with God.

2. 'Tis everlasting peace!
    Sure as Jehovah's name;
  'Tis stable as His steadfast throne,
    For evermore the same.

3. The cross still stands unchanged,
    Though heaven is now His home,
  The mighty stone is rolled away,
    But yonder is His tomb.

4. And yonder is my peace,
    The grave of all my woes!
  I know the Son of God has come,
    I know He died and rose.

5. I know He liveth now.
    At God's right hand above,
  I know the throne on which He sits,
    I know His truth and love.
                                    Bonar.

FAITH.

C. M.
## 114.
T. 14.

How sweet the name of Jesus sounds
  In a believer's ear;
It soothes his sorrows, heals his wounds,
  And drives away his fear.

2. It makes the wounded spirit whole,
  And calms the troubled breast;
'Tis manna to the hungry soul,
  And to the weary rest.

3. Jesus, the Rock on which I build,
  My Shield and Hiding-place,
My never-failing Treasury, fill'd
  With boundless stores of grace:

4. Jesus, my Shepherd, Saviour, Friend,
  My Prophet, Priest and King;
My Lord, my Life, my Way, my End,
  Accept the praise I bring.

5. Weak is the effort of my heart,
  And cold my warmest thought;
But when I see Thee as Thou art,
  I'll praise Thee as I ought.

6. Till then I would Thy love proclaim
  With every fleeting breath;
And may the music of Thy name
  Refresh my soul in death.

*Newton.*

C. M.
## 115.
T. 14.

For ever here my rest shall be
  Close to Thy pierced side;
This all my hope and all my plea,
  For me the Saviour died.

FAITH.

2. My dying Saviour and my God,
    Fountain for guilt and sin!
Sprinkle me ever with Thy blood,
    And cleanse, and keep me clean.

3. Wash me, and make me thus Thine own;
    Wash me, and mine Thou art:
Wash me, but not my feet alone,
    My hands, my head, my heart.

4. The atonement of Thy blood apply,
    Till faith to sight improve;
Till hope in full fruition die,
    And all my soul be love.

C. Wesley.

6s. & 4s.

### 116.

My faith looks up to Thee,
Thou Lamb of Calvary,
    Saviour divine!
Now hear me while I pray,
Take all my guilt away,
Oh, let me from this day
    Be wholly Thine.

2. May Thy rich grace impart
Strength to my fainting heart;
    My zeal inspire:
As Thou hast died for me,
Oh, may my love to Thee,
Pure, warm and changeless be,
    A living fire.

3. While life's dark maze I tread,
And griefs around me spread,
    Be Thou my Guide:
Bid darkness turn to day,
Wipe sorrow's tears away,
Nor let me ever stray
    From Thee aside.

FAITH.

4. When ends life's transient dream,
When death's cold, sullen stream
    Shall o'er me roll,
Blest Saviour, then, in love,
Fear and distrust remove,
O bear me safe above,
    A ransom'd soul.

Ray Palmer.

## 117.

L. M.  T. 22.

Jesus, my all, to heaven is gone;
He whom I fix my hopes upon:
His track I see, and I'll pursue
The narrow way, till Him I view.

2. The way the holy prophets went,
The way that leads from banishment,
The King's highway of holiness,
I'll go, for all His paths are peace.

3. This is the way I long had sought,
And mourn'd because I found it not;
My grief a burden long had been,
Oppress'd with unbelief and sin.

4. The more I strove against their power,
I sinn'd and stumbled but the more;
Till late I heard my Saviour say,
"Come hither, soul, I am the way."

5. Lo! glad I come, and Thou blest Lamb,
Shalt take me to Thee as I am;
Nothing but sin I Thee can give;
Nothing but love I shall receive.

6. Then will I tell to sinners round,
What a dear Saviour I have found;
I'll point to Thy redeeming blood,
And say, "Behold the way to God."

Cennick.

FAITH.

S. M.

## 118.

T. 582.

Not what these hands have done
    Can save this guilty soul;
Not what this toiling flesh has borne
    Can make my spirit whole.

2. Not what I feel or do,
    Can give me peace with God;
Not all my prayers and sighs and tears
    Can bear my awful load.

3. Thy grace alone, O God,
    To me can pardon speak,
Thy power alone, O Son of God,
    Can this sore bondage break.

4. No other work save Thine,
    No meaner blood will do;
No strength save that which is divine,
    Can bear me safely through.

5. I bless the Christ of God;
    I rest on love divine;
And with unfaltering lip and heart,
    I call this Saviour mine.

6. I praise the God of grace,
    I trust His truth and might;
He calls me His, I call Him mine,
    My God, my joy, my light.

7. 'Tis He who saveth me,
    And freely pardon gives,
I love because He loveth me,
    I live, because He lives.

8. My life with Him is hid,
    My death has passed away,
My clouds have melted into light,
    My midnight into day.

Bonar.

## 119.

I lay my sins on Jesus,
  The spotless Lamb of God,
He bears them all, and frees us
  From the accursed load.
I bring my guilt to Jesus
  To wash my crimson stains
White in His blood most precious,
  Till not a spot remains.

2. I lay my wants on Jesus;
  All fullness dwells in Him,
He heals all my diseases,
  He doth my soul redeem.
I lay my griefs on Jesus,
  My burdens and my cares;
He from them all releases,
  He all my sorrows shares.

3. I rest my soul on Jesus,
  This weary soul of mine,
His right hand me embraces,
  I on His breast recline.
I love the name of Jesus,
  Immanuel, Christ the Lord;
Like fragrance on the breezes
  His name abroad is pour'd.

4. I long to be like Jesus,
  Meek, loving, lowly, mild,
I long to be like Jesus,
  The Father's holy Child.
I long to be like Jesus,
  Amid the heavenly throng,
To sing with saints His praises,
  To learn the angels' song.

Bonar.

## IV.—SELF CONSECRATION.

Joshua xxiv. 15.  1 Cor. vi. 20.  Romans xii. 1.

C. M.
### 120.
T. 590.

Present your bodies to the Lord,
  A living sacrifice,
A holy offering unto Him,
  And pleasing to His eyes:
This is a service which ye owe,
  And reasonably due;
For ye are not your own, ye know,
  But Christ hath purchas'd you.

C. M.
### 121.
T. 14.

Lord, take my heart just as it is,
  Set up therein Thy throne:
So shall I love Thee above all,
  And live to Thee alone.

2. I thank Thee, that in mercy Thou
  Hast waken'd me from death,
Arous'd me out of sin's deep sleep,
  And call'd to walk in faith.

3. Complete Thy work and crown Thy grace,
  That I may faithful prove,
And listen to that still small voice,
  Which whispers only love:

4. Which teaches me to know Thy will,
  And gives me power to do:
Which fills my heart with shame, when I
  Do not that will pursue.

## SELF CONSECRATION.

5. This unction may I ever feel,
    This teaching of my Lord,
And learn obedience to Thy voice,
    Thy soft reviving word.

## 122.

7s.                                                                  T. 11.

Grant, most gracious Lamb of God,
Who hast bought me with Thy blood,
That my soul and body be
Quite devoted unto Thee.

2. Jesus, hear my fervent cry,
My whole nature sanctify;
Root out all that is unclean,
Tho' it cause me pungent pain.

3. Gracious Lord, I wish alone
Thine to be, yea, quite Thine own,
And to all eternity
To remain Thy property.                J. Angelus.

## 123.

L. M.*                                                              T. 22.

O happy day, that stays my choice
    On Thee, my Saviour and my God;
Well may this glowing heart rejoice,
    And tell its raptures all abroad.
    [Happy day, happy day,
    When Jesus washed my sins away.]

2. O happy bond, that seals my vows
    To Him who merits all my love!
Let cheerful anthems fill His house,
    While to that sacred shrine I move.

3. 'Tis done—the great transaction's done:
    I am my Lord's, and He is mine;
He drew me, and I followed on,
    Charmed to confess the voice divine.

\* Songs of Devotion, p. 73.

SELF CONSECRATION.

4. Now rest, my long-divided heart,
   Fixed on this blissful centre, rest;
 With ashes who would grudge to part,
   When called on angels' bread to feast?

5. High heaven, that heard the solemn vow,
   That vow renew'd shall daily hear,
 Till in life's latest hour I bow,
   And bless, in death, a bond so dear.
                                    Doddridge.

C. M.                **124.**                T. 14.

Witness, ye men and angels, now,
  Before the Lord we speak;
To Him we make our solemn vow,
  A vow we dare not break:

2. That long as life itself shall last,
     Ourselves to Christ we yield;
   Nor from His cause will we depart,
     Or ever quit the field.

3. We trust not in our native strength,
     But on His grace rely,
   That, with returning wants, the Lord
     Will all our need supply.

4. Lord, guide our doubtful feet aright,
     And keep us in Thy ways,
   And while we turn our vows to prayers,
     Turn Thou our prayers to praise.
                                    Beddome.

C. M.                **125.**                T. 14.

What shall I render to my God
  For all His kindness shown?
My feet shall visit Thine abode,
  My songs address Thy throne.

## SELF CONSECRATION.

2. Among the saints, that fill Thine house,
    My offerings shall be paid;
There shall my zeal perform the vows
    My soul in anguish made.

3. How much is mercy Thy delight,
    Thou ever blessed God!
How dear Thy servants in Thy sight,
    How precious is their blood!

4. How happy all Thy servants are!
    How great Thy grace to me!
My life, which Thou hast made Thy care,
    Lord, I devote to Thee.

5. Now I am Thine, for ever Thine,
    Nor shall my purpose move;
Thy hand has loosed my bonds of pain,
    And bound me with Thy love.

6. Here in Thy courts I leave my vow,
    And Thy rich grace record;
Witness, ye saints, who hear me now,
    If I forsake the Lord.

*Watts.*

C. M. **126.** T. 14.

When we devote our youth to God,
    'Tis pleasing in His eyes:
A flower, when offered in the bud,
    Is no vain sacrifice.

2. To Thee, Almighty God, to Thee,
    Our childhood we resign;
'Twill please us to look back and see
    That our whole lives were Thine.

3. Let the sweet work of prayer and praise
    Employ our youngest breath;
Thus we're prepared for longer days,
    Or fit for early death.

*Watts.*

SELF CONSECRATION.

L. M.

**127.**

T. 22.

Lord, I am Thine, entirely Thine,
Purchas'd and sav'd by blood divine;
With full consent Thine I would be,
And own Thy sovereign right in me.

2. Grant one poor sinner more a place
Among the children of Thy grace;
A wretched sinner, lost to God,
But ransom'd by Immanuel's blood.

3. Thee my new Master now I call,
And consecrate to Thee my all;
Lord, let me live and die to Thee—
Be Thine through all eternity.

*Davies.*

C. M.

**128.**

T. 14.

My God accept my heart this day,
  And make it always Thine,
That I from Thee no more may stray;
  No more from Thee decline.

2. Before the cross of Him who died,
  Behold I prostrate fall;
Let every sin be crucified,
  Let Christ be all in all.

3. Anoint me with Thy heavenly grace,
  Adopt me for Thine own;
That I may see Thy glorious face,
  And worship at Thy throne!

4. May the dear blood once shed for me,
  My blest atonement prove;
That I from first to last may be
  The purchase of Thy love!

5. Let every thought, and work, and word,
   To Thee be ever given;
Then life shall be Thy service, Lord,
   And death the gate of heaven!

C. M.   **129.**   T. 14.

My God! the covenant of Thy love
   Abides for ever sure;
And in its matchless grace I feel
   My happiness secure.

2. Since Thou, the everlasting God,
   My Father art become,
Jesus my Guardian and my Friend,
   And heaven my final home;

3. I welcome all Thy sovereign will,
   For all that will is love;
And when I know not what Thou dost
   I wait the light above.

4. Thy covenant in the darkest gloom
   Shall heavenly rays impart,
And when my eyelids close in death,
   Sustain my fainting heart.

Doddridge.

---

## V.—LOVE.

John x. 11.   1 John iii. 16.   Rev. i. 5, 6.

6s. & 7s. (6 lines.)   **130.**   T. 89.

One there is above all others,
Who deserves the name of Friend;
His is love beyond a brother's,
Costly, free, and knows no end:
They who once His kindness prove,
Find it everlasting love.

2. Which of all our friends, to save us,
Could or would have shed his blood?
But our Jesus died to have us
Reconcil'd in Him to God;
This was boundless love indeed;
Jesus is a friend in need.

3. When He liv'd on earth abased,
"Friend of sinners" was His name;
Now, to heavenly glory raised,
He rejoices in the same:
Still He calls them brethren, friends,
And to all their wants attends.

4. Could we bear from one another,
What He daily bears from us?
Yet this glorious Friend and Brother
Loves us, tho' we treat Him thus;
Tho' for good we render ill,
He accounts us brethren still.

5. Oh, for grace our hearts to soften;
Teach us, Lord, at length to love;
We, alas, forget too often,
What a friend we have above:
But when home our souls are brought,
We will love Thee as we ought.

Newton.

C. M.

## 131.

T. 14.

Jesus, Thy love exceeds by far
  The love of earthly friends;
Bestows whate'er the sinner needs,
  Is firm, and never ends.

2. My blessed Saviour, is Thy love
  So bounteous, great, and free?
Behold I give my sinful heart,
  My life, my all to Thee.

LOVE. 121

3. No man of greater love can boast
   Than for his friend to die:
Thou for Thy enemies wast slain;
   What love with Thine can vie?

4. Tho' in the very form of God,
   With heavenly glory crown'd,
Thou wouldst partake of human flesh,
   Beset with troubles round.

5. And now, upon Thy throne above,
   Thy love is still as great:
Well Thou remember'st Calvary,
   Nor canst Thy death forget.

6. O Lord, I'll treasure in my soul
   The memory of Thy love;
And Thy dear name shall still to me
   A grateful odor prove.

*Watts.*

## 132.     T. 90.

Thee will I love, my strength and tower;
My soul with love to Thee inspire;
Thee will I love with all my power;
Thou art alone my soul's desire:
Thee will I love, my King and God;
Shed in my heart Thy love abroad.

2. Ah, why did I so late Thee know,
Thou fairest of the sons of men?
Ah, why did I no sooner go
To Thee who canst relieve my pain?
Asham'd I sigh and inly mourn,
That I so late to Thee did turn.

3. In darkness willingly I stray'd;
I sought Thee, yet from Thee I rov'd;
For wide my wandering thoughts were spread,
Thy creatures more than Thee I lov'd;

LOVE.

And now if more at length I see,
'Tis through Thy light, and comes from Thee.

4. Give to my eyes repenting tears,
Give to my heart chaste, hallow'd fires;
Give to my soul, with filial fears,
The love that all heaven's host inspires;
That all my powers, with all their might,
In Thy sole glory may unite.

J. Angelus.

11s.     **133.**     T. 39.

I'll glory in nothing but only in Jesus,
As wounded and bruised from sin to release us;
For He is my refuge, to Him I'll cleave solely,
Thus can I, like Enoch, in this world live holy.

2. What tho' the world foameth and rageth with fury,
In nought but my crucified Jesus I'll glory:
Beside Him, my Saviour, I'll know nothing ever;
From Him neither trials nor death shall me sever.

3. My Jesus is always desirous to meet me,
Abounding in love, and in mercy to greet me:
Above all I love Him, for He is my treasure;
I humbly adore Him and serve Him with pleasure.

4. My heart's fix'd on Jesus whose love is so tender;
My life and my all unto Him I surrender:
He is and remaineth my soul's meditation,
My faith's only object, till my consummation.

J. Angelus.

7s.     **134.**     T. 11

Dearest Jesus, come to me
And abide eternally;
Friend of needy sinners, come,
Fill and make my heart Thy home.

LOVE.

2. Oftentimes for Thee I sigh,
Nothing else can give me joy;
This is still my cry to Thee:
Dearest Jesus, come to me.

3. Should I in earth's pleasures roll,
None could satisfy my soul;
Thee, O Jesus, I adore,
Thou'rt my pleasure evermore.

4. Jesus, Thee alone I call
My beloved Friend, my All;
Nothing, whatsoe'er it be,
Shall divide my heart with Thee.

J. Angelus.

8s. & 7s. Double.   **135.**   T. 167.

O could we but love that Saviour,
Who loves us so ardently,
As we ought, our souls would ever
Full of joy and comfort be:
If we, by His love excited,
Could ourselves and all forget,
Then with Jesus Christ united,
We should heaven anticipate.

2. Did but Jesus' love and merit
Fill our hearts both night and day,
And the unction of His Spirit
All our thoughts and actions sway:
Might we all be every ready
Cheerfully to testify,
How our spirit, soul, and body
Do in God our Saviour joy.

Zinzendorf.

LOVE.

## 136.

7s.   T. 11.

Hark, my soul, it is the Lord;
'Tis thy Saviour, hear His word;
Jesus speaks, and speaks to thee,
"Say, poor sinner, lov'st thou Me?

2. "I deliver'd thee, when bound,
And when bleeding, heal'd thy wound;
Sought thee wandering, set thee right,
Turn'd thy darkness into light.

3. "Can a woman's tender care
Cease towards the child she bare?
Yea, she may forgetful be,
Yet will I remember thee.

4. "Mine is an unchanging love,
Higher than the heights above,
Deeper than the depths beneath,
Free and faithful, strong as death.

5. "Thou shalt see my glory soon,
When the work of grace is done,
Partner of my throne shalt be;
Say, poor sinner, lov'st thou Me?"

6. Lord, it is my chief complaint,
That my love is weak and faint;
Yet I love thee and adore,
O for grace to love Thee more.

Cowper.

## 137.

C. M.   T. 14.

I love the Lord! He lent an ear,
  When I for help implor'd;
He rescu'd me from all my fear,
  Therefore, I love the Lord.

LOVE.

2. Return, my soul, unto thy rest:
   From God no longer roam;
His hand hath bountifully blest;
   His goodness calls thee home.

3. What shall I render unto Thee,
   My Saviour in distress!
For all Thy benefits to me,
   So great and numberless?

4. This will I do, for Thy love's sake,
   And thus Thy power proclaim:
Salvation's sacred cup I take,
   And call upon Thy name.

5. Thou God of covenanted grace!
   Hear, and record my vow,
While in Thy courts I seek Thy face,
   And at Thine altar bow:—

6. Henceforth myself to Thee I give,
   With single heart and eye,
To walk before Thee while I live,
   And bless Thee when I die.

Montgomery.

## 138. T. 82.

Jesus makes my heart rejoice,
I'm His sheep, and know His voice;
He's a Shepherd kind and gracious,
And His pastures are delicious;
Constant love to me He shows,
Yea, my worthless name He knows.

2. Trusting His mild staff always,
I go in and out in peace;
He will feed me with the treasure
Of His grace in richest measure;
When athirst to Him I cry,
Living water He'll supply,

LOVE.

3. Should not I for gladness leap,
Led by Jesus as His sheep;
For when these blest days are over,
To the arms of my dear Saviour
I shall be convey'd to rest:
Amen, yea, my lot is blest.

Louisa v. Hayn.

C. M.     **139.**     T. 14.

Thou dear Redeemer, dying Lamb!
  We love to hear of Thee;
No music like Thy charming name,
  Nor half so sweet can be:
O may we ever hear Thy voice!
  In mercy to us speak;
And in our priest we will rejoice,
  Thou great Melchizedek!

2. Our Jesus shall be still our theme,
  While in this world we stay;
We'll sing our Jesus' lovely name,
  When all things else decay:
When we appear in yonder cloud,
  With all His favor'd throng,
Then will we sing more sweet, more loud,
  And Christ shall be our song.

Cennick.

C. M.     **140.**     T. 14.

Jesus, I love Thy charming name,
  'Tis music to my ear;
I gladly would Thy praises sound,
  That earth and heaven might hear.

2. Yes, Thou art precious to my soul,
  In Thee is all my trust;
Jewels to me are gaudy toys,
  And gold is sordid dust.

LOVE. 127

3. O may Thy name still cheer my heart,
And shed its fragrance there;
The noblest balm for all its wounds,
The cordial of its care.

4. I'll speak the honors of Thy name,
With my last laboring breath;
When speechless, Thou shalt be my hope,
My joy in life and death.
Doddridge.

C. M.

## 141.

T. 14.

My God, I love Thee! not because
  I hope for heaven thereby:
Nor yet because, if I love not
  I must forever die.

2. But, O my Jesus, Thou didst me
  Upon the cross embrace:
For me didst bear the nails and spear,
  And manifold disgrace;

3. And griefs and torments numberless,
  And sweat of agony;
E'en death itself; and all for one
  Who was Thine enemy.

4. Then, why, O blessed Jesus Christ!
  Should I not love Thee well;
Not for the sake of winning heaven,
  Or of escaping hell.

5. Not with the hope of gaining aught;
  Not seeking a reward;
But, as Thyself hast loved me,
  O ever-loving Lord!

6. E'en so I love Thee, and will love,
  And in Thy praise will sing;
Solely because Thou art my God,
  And my eternal King.
F Xavier.

LOVE.

S. M. Double.  **142.**  T. 582 or 595.

I was a wandering sheep,
  I did not love the fold,
I did not love my Shepherd's voice,
  I would not be controll'd.
I was a wayward child,
  I did not love my home;
I did not love my Father's voice,
  I loved afar to roam.

2. The Shepherd sought His sheep,
  The Father sought His child,
And follow'd me o'er vale and hill,
  O'er deserts waste and wild.
He found me nigh to death,
  Famish'd, and faint and lone;
He bound me with the bands of love,
  And saved the wand'ring one.

3. He spoke in tender love,
  He raised my drooping head;
He gently closed my bleeding wounds,
  My fainting soul He fed.
He wash'd my filth away,
  He made me clean and fair,
He brought me to my home in peace,
  The long-sought wanderer.

4. Jesus my Shepherd is,
  'Twas He that loved my soul,
'Twas He that wash'd me in His blood,
  'Twas He that made me whole.
'Twas He that sought the lost,
  That found the wandering sheep,
'Twas He that brought me to the fold,
  'Tis He that still doth keep.

5. I was a wandering sheep,
  I would not be controll'd;

LOVE.

But now I love my Shepherd's voice,
　I love, I love the fold!
I was a wayward child;
　I once preferr'd to roam,
But now I love my Father's voice;
　I love, I love His home!

*Bonar.*

L. M.　　　　**143.**　　　　T. 22.

I love the Lord who died for me
I love His grace divine and free;
I love the Scriptures, there I read,
Christ loved me, and for me bled.

2. I love His tears and sufferings great,
I love His precious bloody sweat,
I love His blood; were that not spilt,
I could not have been freed from guilt.

3. I love to hear that He was slain,
I love His every grief and pain,
I love to meditate by faith
Upon His meritorious death.

4. I love Mount Calvary, where His love
Stronger than death itself did prove;
I love to walk His dolorous way,
I love the grave where Jesus lay.

5. I love His people and their ways,
I love with them to pray and praise;
I love the Father and the Son,
I love the Spirit He sent down.

6. I love to think the time will come,
When I shall be with Him at home,
And praise Him in eternity:
Then shall my love completed be.

*Cennick.*

LOVE.

L. M. **144.** T. 22.

Love is the theme of saints above;
  Love be the theme of saints below;
Love is of God, for God is love;
  With love let every bosom glow.

2. Love to the Spirit of all grace,
  Love to the Scriptures of all truth;
Love to our whole apostate race.
  Love to the aged, love to youth;

3. Love to each other;—soul and mind,
  And heart and hand with full accord,
In one sweet covenant combined,
  To live and die unto the Lord.

C. M. **145.** T. 14.

How sweet, how heavenly is the sight,
  When those who love the Lord,
In one another's peace delight,
  And so fulfill His word!

2. When each can feel his brother's sigh,
  And with him bear a part;
When sorrow flows from eye to eye,
  And joy from heart to heart;

3. When free from envy, scorn and pride,
  Our wishes all above,
Each can a brother's failings hide,
  And show a brother's love;

4. When love in one delightful stream,
  Through every bosom flows;
When union sweet, and fond esteem,
  In every action glows

LOVE. 131

5. Love is the golden chain, that binds
   The happy souls above;
And he's an heir of heaven that finds
   His spirit fill'd with love.

Swaine.

S. M.     **146.**     T. 582 or 595.

Blest is the tie that binds
Our hearts in Christian love;
The fellowship of kindred minds
Is like to that above.

2. Before our Father's throne
We pour our ardent prayers;
Our fears, our hopes, our aims, are one,
Our comforts and our cares.

3. We share our mutual woes,
Our mutual burdens bear,
And often for each other flows,
The sympathising tear.

4. We're one in Christ our Head,
In Him we grow and thrive;
Nor will He leave us with the dead,
While He remains alive.

5. This glorious hope revives
Our courage by the way;
While each in expectation lives,
And longs to see the day.

Fawcett.

8s. & 7s.     **147.**     T. 16.

Little children, love each other,
   Is the blessed Saviour's rule;
Every little one is brother
   To his mates at Sabbath School.

LOVE.

2. We're all children of one Father,
The great God who reigns above;
Shall we quarrel?—No; much rather
Should we be like Him—all love.

8s. & 7s.         **148.**         T. 76.

Children, do you love each other?
  Are you always kind and true?
Do you always do to others
  As you'd have them do to you?

2. Are you gentle to each other?
  Are you careful day by day,
Not to give offence by actions,
  Or by any thing you say?

3. Little children, love each other;
  Never give another pain;
If your brother speak in anger,
  Answer not in wrath again.

4. Be not selfish to each other;
  Never spoil another's rest;
Strive to make each other happy,
  And you will yourselves be blest.

L. M.         **149.**         T. 22.

The lambs of Jesus:—who are they,
But children that believe and pray,
That keep God's laws, and ask His grace,
And seek a heavenly dwelling-place.

2. The lambs of Jesus:—they are meek,
The words of peace and truth they speak;
To all God's creatures they are kind,
And, like their Lord, of gentle mind.

3. The lambs of Jesus:—oh that we
Might of that blessed number be!
Lord, take us early to Thy love,
And lead us to the fold above.

---

## VI.—JOY AND PRAISE.
### Ps. xxxiv. 1, 3.
### 150.

7s.    T. 11.

Blest are they, supremely blest,
Who of Jesus' grace possess'd,
Cleave to Him by living faith,
Till they shall resign their breath.

2. One with Christ their Head they share
Happiness beyond compare;
Since on Him their hopes they build,
He is their reward and shield.

3. Tho' all earthly joys be fled,
If in Him they trust indeed,
He will be their constant friend,
And protect them to the end.

4. If to Jesus they appeal,
When their faith and courage fail,
He assures them of His love,
Doth their strength in weakness prove.

5. They who simply to Him cleave,
From His fulness grace receive;
And throughout their mortal days
Their employment is His praise.

6. Jesus wipes away their tears,
And their drooping spirits cheers;
They in truth, with heart and voice,
Evermore in Him rejoice.

J. G. Wolf.

## 151.

T. 115.

How great the bliss to be a sheep of Jesus,
And to be guided by His shepherd-staff!
Earth's greatest honors, howsoe'er they please us,
Compar'd to this are vain and empty chaff:
Yea, what this world can never give,
May, thro' the Shepherd's grace, each needy sheep receive.

2. Here is a pasture, rich and never failing,
Here living waters in abundance flow;
None can conceive the grace with them prevailing,
Who Jesus' shepherd-voice obey and know:
He banishes all fear and strife,
And leads them gently on to everlasting life.

3. Whoe'er would spend his days in lasting pleasure,
Must come to Christ, and join His flock with speed;
Here is a feast prepar'd, rich beyond measure,
The world meanwhile on empty husks must feed:
Those souls may share in every good
Whose Shepherd doth possess the treasuries of God.

J. J. Rambach.

C. M.

## 152.

T. 14.

If Christ is mine, then all is mine,
And more than angels know;
Both present things, and things to come,
And grace and glory too.

2. If He is mine, then though He frown,
He never will forsake;
His chastisements all work for good,
And but His love bespeak.

3. If He is mine I need not fear
The rage of earth and hell;
He will support my feeble frame,
And all their power repel.

## JOY AND PRAISE.

4. If He is mine, let friends forsake,
And earthly comforts flee,
He, the dispenser of all good,
Is more than all to me.

5. If He is mine, unharm'd I pass
Thro' death's tremendous vale,
He'll be my comfort and my stay,
When heart and flesh shall fail.

6. ·Let Christ assure me He is mine,
I nothing want beside;
My soul shall at the fountain live,
When all the streams are dried.

*Beddome.*

7s Double.  **153.**  T. 205.

Happiness, delightful name,
Where may it be found, O where?
Learning, pleasure, wealth, and fame,
All confess, It is not here:—
Jesus crucified to know,
This is happiness below;
Him to see, adore, and love,
This is happiness above.

*Toplady.*

C. M.  **154.**  T. 14.

My God, the spring of all my joys,
  The life of my delights;
The glory of my brightest days,
  And comfort of my nights;—

2. In darkest shades, if Thou appear,
  My dawning is begun:
Thou art my soul's bright morning-star,
  And Thou my rising sun.

3. The opening heavens around me shine
   With beams of sacred bliss,
When Jesus shows His mercies mine,
   And whispers I am His.

Watts.

## 155.

T. 341.

Thou, Jesus, art our King;
   Thy ceaseless praise we sing:
Praise shall our glad tongues employ,
   Praise o'erflow the grateful soul,
While we vital breath enjoy,
   While eternal ages roll.

2. Thou hast o'erthrown the foe,
   God's kingdom fix'd below:
Conqueror of all adverse power,
   Thou heaven's gates hast open'd wide;
Thou Thine own dost lead secure,
   And to life eternal guide.

3. Above the starry sky
   Thou reign'st, enthron'd on high;
Prostrate at Thy feet we fall:
   Power supreme to Thee is giv'n,
As the righteous Judge of all
   Sons of earth and hosts of heaven.

4. Arise, exert Thy power,
   Thou glorious Conqueror;
Help us to obtain the prize,
   Help us well to close our race;
That with Thee above the skies
   Endless joys we may possess.

J. Angelus.

## JOY AND PRAISE.

C. M.

## 156.

T. 14.

Come let us join our cheerful songs
   With angels round the throne:
Ten thousand thousands are their tongues,
   But all their joys are one.

2. "Worthy the Lamb that died," they cry,
   "To be exalted thus;"
"Worthy the Lamb," our hearts reply,
   "For He was slain for us."

3. Jesus is worthy to receive
   Honor and power divine;
And blessings more than we can give,
   Be, Lord, for ever Thine.

4. The whole creation join in one,
   To bless the sacred name
Of Him that sits upon the throne,
   And to adore the Lamb.

*Watts.*

L. M.

## 157.

T. 22.

Awake, my soul, in joyful lays,
And sing Thy great Redeemer's praise,
He justly claims a song from Thee,—
His loving-kindness, oh, how free!

2. He saw me ruin'd in the fall,
Yet loved me notwithstanding all;
He saved me from my lost estate,—
His loving-kindness, oh, how great!

3. When trouble like a gloomy cloud,
Has gather'd thick, and thunder'd loud,
He near my soul has always stood,—
His loving-kindness, oh, how good!

JOY AND PRAISE.

4. Often I feel my sinful heart
Prone from my Saviour to depart;
But though I oft have Him forgot,
His loving-kindness changes not.

5. Soon shall I pass the gloomy vale,
Soon all my mortal powers must fail:
Oh, may my last expiring breath
His loving-kindness sing in death.

Medley

S. M.     **158.**     T. 595.

Awake, and sing the song
  Of Moses and the Lamb;
Wake every heart and every tongue,
  To praise the Saviour's name.

2. Sing of His dying love,
  Sing of His rising power;
Sing how He intercedes above
  For us whose sins He bore.

3. Ye pilgrims on the road
  To Zion's city, sing:
Rejoice ye in the Lamb of God,
  In Christ, the eternal King.

4. Soon shall we hear Him say,
  "Ye blessed children, come;"
Soon will He call us hence away
  To our eternal home.

5. There shall our raptur'd tongues
  His endless praise proclaim,
And sweeter voices tune the song,
  Of Moses and the Lamb.

Hammond.

## JOY AND PRAISE.

S. M.

### 159.

T. 595.

To God the only wise,
  Our Saviour and our King,
Let all the saints below the skies
  Their humble praises bring.

2. 'Tis His almighty love,
  His counsel and His care,
Preserve us safe from sin and death,
  And every hurtful snare.

3. He will present our souls,
  Unblemish'd and complete,
Before the glory of His face,
  With joys divinely great.

4. The Saviour's ransom'd race
  Shall meet around the throne,
Extol Him for His saving grace,
  And make His wonders known.

5. To our Redeemer-God,
  Wisdom and power belong;
Immortal crowns of majesty,
  And heaven's eternal song.

*Watts.*

L. M.

### 160.

T. 22.

Now to the Lord a noble song!
Awake, my soul! awake, my tongue!
Hosanna to the eternal name!
And all His boundless love proclaim.

2. See where it shines in Jesus' face,
The brightest image of His grace;
God, in the person of His Son,
Has all His mightiest works outdone.

JOY AND PRAISE.

3. Grace!—'tis a sweet, a charming theme;
My thoughts rejoice at Jesus' name;
Ye angels, dwell upon the sound;
Ye heavens, reflect it to the ground.

4. Oh, may I reach that happy place,
Where He unveils His lovely face,
Where all His beauties you behold,
And sing His name to harps of gold.

*Watts.*

P. M.*

## 161.

Children of Jerusalem
Sang the praise of Jesus' name;
Children, too, of later days,
Join to sing the Saviour's praise.
 Hark! while infant voices sing
 Loud hosannas to our King.

2. We have often heard and read
What the royal psalmist said:
Babes, and sucklings' artless lays
Shall proclaim the Saviour's praise.
 Hark! &c.

3. We are taught to love the Lord,
We are taught to read His word,
We are taught the way to heaven:
Praise to God for all be given.
 Hark! &c.

4. Parents, teachers, old and young,
All unite to swell the song;
Higher and yet higher rise,
Till hosannas reach the skies.
 Hark! &c.

* P. S. S. Coll., p. 211.

## JOY AND PRAISE.    141

11s.    **162.**    T. 39.

Ye servants of God your great Master proclaim,
And publish abroad His most excellent name:
The name all victorious of Jesus extol,
His kingdom is glorious, He rules over all.

2. God ruleth in heaven, almighty to save,
And yet He is with us, His presence we have:
The great congregation His triumphs shall sing,
Ascribing salvation to Jesus our King.

3. Salvation be brought unto God on the throne,
Let all sing rejoicing, and honor the Son;
The praises of Jesus the angels proclaim,
Fall down on their faces and worship the Lamb.

4. Then let us adore Him and give Him His right,
All glory, and power, and wisdom, and might,
And honor, and blessing, with angels above,
And thanks never ceasing for infinite love.
                                C. Wesley.

7s.    **163.**    T. 1L

Children of the heavenly King!
As ye journey, sweetly sing!
Sing your Saviour's worthy praise,
Glorious in His works and ways!

2. We are travelling home to God,
In the way the fathers trod:
They are happy now, and we
Soon their happiness shall see.

3. Foes are round us, but we stand
On the borders of our land:
Jesus, God's exalted Son,
Bids us undismayed go on.

JOY AND PRAISE.

4. Onward then we gladly press
Through this earthly wilderness:
Only, Lord, our Leader be,
And we still will follow Thee.

Cennick.

7s. & 6s.

**164.**

T. 151.

Come let us sing of Jesus,
  While hearts and accents blend;
Come, let us sing of Jesus,
  The sinner's only friend:
His holy soul rejoices,
  Amid the choirs above,
To hear our youthful voices
  Exulting in His love.

2. We love to sing of Jesus,
  Who wept our path along;
We love to sing of Jesus,
  The tempted and the strong:
None who besought His healing,
  He pass'd unheeded by:
And still retains His feeling
  For us above the sky.

3. We love to sing of Jesus,
  Who died our souls to save;
We love to sing of Jesus,
  Triumphant o'er the grave;
And in our hour of danger
  We'll trust His love alone,
Who once slept in a manger,
  And now sits on the throne.

4. Then let us sing of Jesus,
  While yet on earth we stay,
And hope to sing of Jesus
  Throughout eternal day:

## JOY AND PRAISE.

For those who here confess Him,
  He will in heaven confess;
And faithful hearts that bless Him,
  He will forever bless.

G. W. Bethune.

8s. & 7s. Double.     **165.**     T. 167.

Who shall sing, if not the children?
  Did not Jesus die for them?
May they not, with other jewels,
  Sparkle in His diadem?
Why to them were voices given—
  Bird-like voices, sweet and clear—
Why, unless the song of heaven
  They begin and practise here?

2. There's a choir of infant songsters,
  White-robed, round the Saviour's throne;
Angels cease, and waiting listen;
  Oh! 'tis sweeter than their own.
Faith can hear the rapturous choral,
  When her ear is upward turned;
Is it not the same, perfected,
  Which upon the earth they learned?

3. Jesus, when on earth sojourning,
  Loved them with a wondrous love;
And will He, to heaven returning,
  Faithless to His blessing prove?
Oh! they cannot sing too early!
  Stand, Oh, stand not in their way!
Birds do sing while day is breaking—
  Tell me, then, why should not they?

7s.     **166.**     T. 11.

Songs of praise the angels sang,
Heaven with hallelujahs rang,
When Jehovah's work begun,
When He spake and it was done.

JOY AND PRAISE.

2. Songs of praise awoke the morn,
When the Prince of peace was born;
Songs of praise arose, when He
Captive led captivity.

3. Saints below, with heart and voice,
Still in songs of praise rejoice;
Learning here, by faith and love,
Songs of praise to sing above.

4. Borne upon their latest breath,
Songs of praise shall conquer death,
Then, amid eternal joy,
Songs of praise their powers employ.
Montgomery.

S. M.  **167.**  T. 582 or 595

Come, ye who love the Lord,
  And let your joys be known;
Join in a song with sweet accord,
  And thus surround the throne.

2. Let those refuse to sing,
  Who never knew our God;
But servants of the heavenly King
  Should speak their joys abroad.

3. The men of grace have found
  Glory begun below;
Celestial fruits on earthly ground
  From faith and hope may grow.

4. The hill of Zion yields
  A thousand sacred sweets,
Before we reach the heavenly fields
  Or walk the golden streets.

JOY AND PRAISE.

5. Then let our songs abound,
   And every tear be dry;
We're marching through Immanuel's ground,
   To fairer worlds on high.

*Watts.*

7s.

## 168.

T. 11.

Glory to the Father give,
God in whom we move and live;
Children's prayers He deigns to hear,
Children's songs delight His ear.

2. Glory to the Son we bring,
Christ our Prophet, Priest and King;
Children, raise your sweetest strain
To the Lamb, for He was slain.

3. Glory to the Holy Ghost;
Be this day a Pentecost:
Children's minds may He inspire,
Touch their tongues with holy fire,

4. Glory in the highest be
To the blessed Trinity,
For the Gospel from above,
For the word, that "God is love."

*Montgomery.*

6s. & 4s.

## 169.

Come, thou Almighty King,
Help us Thy name to sing,
   Help us to praise!
Father, all glorious,
O'er all victorious,
Come and reign over us,
   Ancient of days!

JOY AND PRAISE.

2. Jesus our Lord, arise,
Scatter our enemies!
　Now make them fall!
Let Thine almighty aid
Our sure defence be made,
Our souls on Thee be stay'd:
　Lord, hear our call!

3. Come, Thou incarnate Word,
Gird on Thy mighty sword;
　Our prayer attend!
Come, and Thy people bless;
Come, give Thy word success;
Spirit of holiness,
　On us descend!

Maddan.

8s. 7s. & 4s.　　**170.**　　T. 585.

Praise to Thee, O Lord, we render,
　For Thy love in Jesus shown:
May that love, so strong and tender,
　Bind us fast to Him alone;
　　Now and ever :‖:
Gather us among Thine own.

2. By Thy Spirit's power renewing
　May our hearts be purified;
And our wills to Thine subduing,
　May His grace control and guide;
　　Now and ever, :‖:
In our hearts may He abide.

3. Visit us with Thy salvation,
　Guard us by Thy power divine,
Make our house Thy habitation,
　Make each heart Thy peaceful shrine,
　　Now and ever :‖:
Make us, Lord, and keep us Thine.

## 171.

T. 230

Praises, thanks, and adoration
Be given to God without cessation,
To Jesus Christ our gracious Lord:
For His mercy, love, and favor
To us, His flock, endure forever;
Bless, bless His name with one accord;
To God, the Father, Son,
And Spirit, Three in One,
Hallelujah:
In highest strain
Praise the Lamb slain:
Let heaven and earth reply, Amen.

J. Swertner.

---

### VII.—PRAYER.

Ps. 1. 15.   John xiv. 13, 14.   Romans xii. 12.

C. M.
## 172.
T. 14.

Prayer is the soul's sincere desire,
  Unutter'd or express'd;
The motion of a hidden fire
  That trembles in the breast.

2. Prayer is the burden of a sigh,
  The falling of a tear,
The upward glancing of an eye
  When none but God is near.

3. Prayer is the simplest form of speech
  That infant lips can try;
Prayer, the sublimest strains that reach
  The Majesty on high.

4. Prayer is the Christian's vital breath,
  The Christian's native air;
His watchword at the gates of death—
  He enters heaven with prayer.

5. Prayer is the contrite sinner's voice,
   Returning from his ways;
While angels in their songs rejoice,
   And cry, "Behold, he prays!"

6. O Thou, by whom we come to God,
   The Life, the Truth, the Way;
The path of prayer Thyself hast trod:
   Lord, teach us how to pray!

Montgomery.

7s.
## 173.
T. 11.

Come, my soul, thy suit prepare,
Jesus loves to answer prayer;
He himself hath bid Thee pray,
And sends none unheard away.

2. Thou art coming to a King,
Large petitions with thee bring;
For His grace and power are such,
None can ever ask too much.

3. Lord, I will not let Thee go,
Till the blessing Thou bestow:
Oh, do not my suit disdain;
None shall seek Thy face in vain.

J. Newton.

S. M.
## 174.
T. 595.

Behold the throne of grace,
   The promise calls me near,
There Jesus shows His cheering face,
   And waits to answer prayer.

2. That rich, atoning blood,
   Which sprinkled round I see,
Provides for those who come to God
   An all-prevailing plea.

PRAYER. 149

3. My soul, ask what thou wilt,
 Thou canst not be too bold;
Since His own blood for thee was spilt,
 What else can He withhold?

4. Beyond thy utmost wants
 His love and power can bless;
To praying souls He always grants
 More than they can express.

5. Since 'tis the Lord's command,
 My mouth I open wide:
Lord, open Thou Thy bounteous hand,
 That I may be supplied.

6. My soul, believe and pray,
 Without a doubt believe:
Whate'er we ask in God's own way,
 We surely shall receive.

7. Here stands the promise fair,
 For God cannot repent,
To fervent, persevering prayer,
 He'll every blessing grant.

J. Newton.

L. M. **175.** T. 22.

What various hindrances we meet
In coming to a mercy seat;
Yet who that knows the worth of prayer,
But wishes to be often there.

2. Prayer makes the darken'd cloud withdraw;
Prayer climbs the ladder Jacob saw;
Gives exercise to faith and love;
Brings every blessing from above.

3. Restraining prayer, we cease to fight;
Prayer makes the Christian's armor bright;
And Satan trembles when he sees
The weakest saint upon his knees.

4. While Moses stood with arms spread wide,
Success was found on Israel's side;
But when through weariness they fail'd,
That moment Amalek prevail'd.

5. Have you no words? Ah, think again;
Words flow apace when you complain,
And fill your fellow-creature's ear
With the sad tale of all your care.

6. Were half the breath thus vainly spent,
To heaven in supplication sent,
Your cheerful song would oftener be,
"Hear what the Lord has done for me."

*Cowper.*

7s. & 6s. **176.** T. 151.

Go when the morning shineth,
  Go when the moon is bright,
Go when the eve declineth,
  Go in the hush of night;
Go with pure mind and feeling—
  Send earthly thoughts away—
And in thy chamber kneeling,
  Do thou in secret pray.

2. Oh! not a joy or blessing
  With this can we compare,
The power that He has given us,
  To pour our souls in prayer;
Then for thyself and neighbor
  A blessing humbly claim,
And link with each petition
  Thy great Redeemer's name.

3. Or, if 'tis e'er denied thee
  In solitude to pray,
Should holy thoughts come o'er thee
  When friends are round thy way;

PRAYER.

E'en then the silent breathing
  Thy spirit lifts above,
Will reach the throne of glory,
  Where dwells eternal love.

4. Oh! not a joy or blessing
  With this can we compare,
The grace our Father gives us,
  To pour our souls in prayer;
Whene'er thou art in sadness,
  Before His footstool fall;
Remember, too, in gladness,
  His love, who gave thee all.
Mrs Simpson.

## 177.

L. M.                                       T. 22.

My Father, when I come to Thee,
I would not only bend the knee,
But with my spirit seek Thy face,
With my whole heart desire thy grace.

2. I plead the name of Thy dear Son;
All He has said, all He has done:
Oh, may I feel His love for me,
Who died from sin to set me free!

3. My Saviour, guide me with Thine eye;
My sins forgive, my wants supply;
With favor crown my youthful days,
And my whole life shall speak Thy praise.

4. Thy Holy Spirit, Lord, impart;
Impress Thy likeness on my heart;
May I obey Thy truth in love,
Till raised to dwell with Thee above.

## VIII.—CONFESSION OF CHRIST.

Matt. x. 32, 33.  1 John iv. 5.

8s. & 7s.

# 178.

T. 167.

Jesus, I my cross have taken,
All to leave and follow Thee;
Naked, poor, despis'd, forsaken,
Thou, from hence, my All shalt be;
Perish every fond ambition,
All I've sought, or hop'd, or known;
Yet how rich is my condition,
God and heaven are still my own.

2. Let the world despise and leave me,
They have left my Saviour too:
Human hearts and looks deceive me—
Thou art not, like them, untrue;
And whilst Thou shalt smile upon me,
God of wisdom, love, and might,
Foes may hate, and friends disown me,
Show Thy face, and all is bright.

3. Go, then, earthly fame and treasure;
Come, disaster, scorn, and pain:
In Thy service pain is pleasure,
With Thy favor loss is gain;
Man may trouble and distress me,
'Twill but drive me to Thy breast;
Life with trials hard may press me,
Heaven will bring the sweeter rest.

4. Soul, then know thy full salvation;
Rise o'er sin, and fear, and care;
Joy to find in every station,
Something still to do or bear;

## CONFESSION OF CHRIST. 153

Think what Spirit dwells within thee,
Think what Father's smiles are thine;
Think that Jesus died to win thee:
Child of heaven, canst thou repine?

5. Haste thee on from grace to glory,
Arm'd by faith, and wing'd by prayer;
Heaven's eternal day's before thee;
God's own hand shall guide thee there;
Soon shall close thy earthly mission,
Soon shall pass thy pilgrim days:
Hope shall change to full fruition,
Faith to sight, and prayer to praise.

*Lyte.*

L. M. **179.** T. 22.

Jesus! and shall it ever be,
A mortal man asham'd of Thee!
Asham'd of Thee, whom angels praise,
Whose glories shine through endless days?

2. Asham'd of Jesus! sooner far
Let evening blush to own a star:
He sheds the beams of light divine
O'er this benighted soul of mine.

3. Asham'd of Jesus!—just as soon
Let midnight be asham'd of noon:
'Tis midnight with my soul, till He,
Bright morning-star, bids darkness flee.

4. Asham'd of Jesus! that dear Friend
On whom my hopes of heaven depend?
No, when I blush, be this my shame,
That I no more revere His name!

5. Asham'd of Jesus!—yes, I may,
When I've no guilt to wash away;
No tear to wipe; no good to crave;
No fear to quell; no soul to save.

6. Till then—nor is my boasting vain—
Till then I boast a Saviour slain!
And oh! may this my glory be,
That Christ is not asham'd of me.

Gregg.

C. M.
### 180.
T. 14.

I'm not ashamed to own my Lord,
  Or to defend His cause,
Maintain the honor of His word,
  The glory of His cross.

2. Jesus, my God! I know His name,
  His name is all my trust;
Nor will He put my soul to shame,
  Nor let my hope be lost.

3. Firm as His throne His promise stands,
  And He can well secure
What I've committed to His hands,
  Till the decisive hour.

4. Then will He own my worthless name
  Before His Father's face,
And in the new Jerusalem
  Appoint my soul a place.

Watts.

### 181.
T. 587.

O tell me no more
Of this world's vain store,
The time for such trifles with me now is o'er.

2. A country I've found,
Where true joys abound;
To dwell I'm determin'd on that happy ground.

3. The souls that believe,
In paradise live:
And me in that number will Jesus receive.

CONFESSION OF CHRIST. 155

4. My soul, don't delay,
He calls thee away:
Rise, follow thy Saviour, and bless the glad day.

5. No mortal doth know
What he can bestow,
What light, strength, and comfort; go, follow Him, **go**.

6. Perhaps with the aim
To honor His name,
I may do some service, poor dust tho' I am.

7. Yet this is confess'd,
I count it most bless'd,
As at the beginning, in Him to find rest.

8. And when I'm to die,
Receive me, I'll cry,
For Jesus hath loved me, I cannot tell why.

9. But this I do find,
We two are so joined,
He'll not live in glory and leave me behind.

10. Lo, this is the race
I'm running thro' grace
Henceforth, till admitted to see my Lord's face.
J. Gambold.

C. M. **182.** T. 14.

Am I a soldier of the cross?
A follower of the Lamb?
And shall I fear to own His cause,
Or blush to speak His name?

2. Must I be carried to the skies
On flowery beds of ease?
While others fought to win the prize,
And sail'd through bloody seas?

CONFESSION OF CHRIST.

3. Are there no foes for me to face?
   Must I not stem the flood?
Is this vile world a friend of grace,
   To help me on to God?

4. Sure, I must fight, if I would reign;
   Increase my courage, Lord;
I'll bear the toil, endure the pain,
   Supported by Thy word.

5. Thy saints, in all this glorious war,
   Shall conquer, though they die;
They view the triumph from afar,
   With faith's discerning eye.
                                    Watts.

C. M.                **183.**                T. 14.

Hail church of Christ, bought with His blood!
   The world I freely leave;
Ye children of the living God,
   Me in your tents receive.

2. Bride of the Lamb, I'm one in heart
   With Thee, thro' boundless grace,
And I will never from Thee part;
   This bond shall never cease.

3. Closely I'll follow Christ with thee,
   I'll go thy safest road;
Thy people shall my people be,
   And thine shall be my God.

4. And am I, Jesus, one of those
   Who in thy fold have place?
Who, gather'd round the erected cross,
   Enjoy redeeming grace?

5. O yes, nor would I change my lot
   For an archangel's throne;
By grace I'll keep the place I've got,
   To Thee I'll live alone.
                                    Cennick.

CONFESSION OF CHRIST.

## 184.

S. M.   T. 595.

A charge to keep I have,
  A God to glorify;
A never-dying soul to save,
  And fit it for the sky.

2. To serve the present age,
  My calling to fulfill,—
Oh, may it all my powers engage,
  To do my Master's will.

3. Arm me with jealous care,
  As in Thy sight to live;
And oh, Thy servant, Lord, prepare,
  The strict account to give.

4. Help me to watch and pray,
  And on Thyself rely
Assured, if I my trust betray,
  I shall forever die.

C. Wesley.

## 185.

S. M.   T. 582.

My soul, be on thy guard.
  Ten thousand foes arise;
The hosts of sin are pressing hard
  To draw thee from the skies.

2. Oh, watch, and fight, and pray;
  The battle ne'er give o'er;
Renew it boldly every day,
  And help divine implore.

3. Ne'er think the vict'ry won,
  Nor lay thine armor down;
The work of faith will not be done.
  Till thou obtain the crown.

4. Then persevere till death
Shall bring thee to thy God;
He'll take thee, at thy parting breath,
To His divine abode.

Heath.

L. M.

## 186.

T. 22.

Stand up, my soul, shake off thy fears,
And gird the gospel-armor on;
March to the gates of endless joy,
Where Jesus thy great Captain's gone.

2. Hell and thy sins resist thy course;
But hell and sin are vanquished foes;
Thy Saviour nail'd them to the cross,
And sung the triumph when He rose.

3. Then let my soul march boldly on,
Press forward to the heavenly gate;
There peace and joy eternal reign,
And glittering robes for conquerors wait.

4. There shall I wear a starry crown,
And triumph in almighty grace,
While all the armies of the skies
Join in my glorious Leader's praise.

Watts.

7s. & 6s.

## 187.

T. 151.

Stand up!—stand up for Jesus!
 Ye soldiers of the cross;
Lift high His royal banner,
 It must not suffer loss:
From victory unto victory
 His army shall be led,
Till every foe is vanquished,
 And Christ is Lord indeed.

2. Stand up!—stand up for Jesus!
The trumpet call obey;

Forth to the mighty conflict
  In this His glorious day;
"Ye that are men, now serve Him"
  Against unnumbered foes;
Your courage rise with danger,
  And strength to strength oppose.

3. Stand up!—stand up for Jesus!
  Stand in His strength alone;
The arm of flesh will fail you—
  Ye dare not trust your own;
Put on the Gospel armor,
  And, watching unto prayer,
Where duty calls or danger,
  Be never wanting there.

4. Stand up!—stand up for Jesus!
  The strife will not be long;
This day the noise of battle,
  The next the victor's song:
To him that overcometh,
  A crown of life shall be;
He with the King of glory
  Shall reign eternally.      *Duffield.*

---

## IX.—PATIENCE AND TRUST.

Psalm xviii. 2. 1 Peter iv. 12; v. 6.

### 188.

*7s. & 6s.*                                *T. 151.*

Is God my strong Salvation,
  No enemy I fear;
He hears my supplication,
  Dispelling all my care:
If He, my Head and Master,
  Defend me from above,
What pain or what disaster
  Can part me from His love?

## PATIENCE AND TRUST.

2. Should earth lose its foundation,
   He stands my lasting rock;
No temporal desolation
   Shall give my love a shock:
I'll cleave to Christ my Saviour,
   No object, small or great,
Nor height, nor depth, shall ever
   Me from Him separate.

P. Gerhard.

## 189.

7s. Double.                          T. 206.

To the hills I lift mine eyes,
To the everlasting hills;
Thence I draw divine supplies,
Thus my soul new vigor fills;
Faithful is His promis'd word;
Help, while yet I ask, is giv'n;
Giv'n by Him, the sovereign Lord,
Who hath made both earth and heaven.

2. Not the powers of earth or hell
E'er thy Guardian can surprise;
Careless slumber cannot steal
Over His all-seeing eyes;
He is Israel's sure defence;
Israel all His care shall prove;
Kept by watchful Providence,
Borne by ever-waking love.

3. Thee, on evil's baleful day,
Scorching sun shall never smite;
Nor the moon with chilling ray
Ever blast thee through the night:
Safe from known or secret foes,
Free from sin and Satan's thrall,
When the flesh, earth, hell oppose,
God shall keep thee safe from all.

C. Wesley.

## 190.

7s. Double.  T. 205.

Jesus, lover of my soul,
  Let me to Thy bosom fly,
While the raging billows roll,
  While the tempest still is high:
Hide me, O my Saviour, hide,
  Till the storm of life is past;
Safe into the haven guide:
  O receive my soul at last.

2. Other refuge have I none,
  Hangs my helpless soul on Thee;
Leave, O leave me not alone,
  Still support and comfort me:
All my trust on Thee is stay'd,
  All my help from Thee I bring:
Cover my defenceless head
  With the shadow of Thy wing.

3. Wilt Thou not regard my call?
  Wilt thou not accept my prayer?
Lo! I sink, I faint, I fall!
  Lo! on Thee I cast my care!
Reach me out Thy gracious hand!
  While I of Thy strength receive,
Hoping against hope I stand,
  Dying and behold I live!

4. Thou, O Christ, art all I want,
  All in all in Thee I find;
Raise the fallen, cheer the faint,
  Heal the sick, and lead the blind:
Just and holy is Thy name,
  I am all unrighteousness;
Vile and full of sin I am,
  Thou art full of truth and grace.

5. Plenteous grace with Thee is found,
  Grace to pardon all my sin;

PATIENCE AND TRUST.

Let the healing streams abound,
  Make and keep me pure within!
Thou of life the fountain art,
  Freely let me take of Thee;
Spring Thou up within my heart!
  Rise to all eternity!

C. Wesley.

8s. 7s. & 4s.
### 191.
T. 585.

Guide me, O Thou great Jehovah!
  Pilgrim through this barren land:
I am weak—but Thou art mighty;
  Hold me with Thy powerful hand;
    Bread of heaven! :||:
Feed me till I want no more.

2. Open now the crystal fountain,
  Whence the healing waters flow;
Let the fiery, cloudy pillar,
  Lead me all my journey through;
    Strong Deliv'rer! :||:
Be Thou still my strength and shield.

3. When I tread the verge of Jordan,
  Bid my anxious fears subside;
Bear me through the swelling current,
  Land me safe on Canaan's side;
    Songs of praise :||:
I will ever give to Thee.

Wm. Williams.

6s. & 4s.
### 192.

Nearer, my God to Thee,
  Nearer to Thee!
E'en though it be a cross
  That raiseth me;
Still all my song shall be,
Nearer, my God, to Thee,
  Nearer to Thee!

2. Though, like the wanderer,
    The sun gone down,
Darkness be over me,
    My rest a stone:
Yet in my dreams I'd be
Nearer, my God to Thee,
    Nearer to Thee!

3. There let the way appear,
    Steps unto heaven;
All that Thou sendest me,
    In mercy given;
Angels to beckon me
Nearer, my God, to Thee,
    Nearer to Thee!

4. Then with my waking thoughts,
    Bright with Thy praise,
Out of my stony griefs,
    Bethel I'll raise;
So by my woes to be
Nearer, my God, to Thee,
    Nearer to Thee!

5. And when, on joyful wing,
    Cleaving the sky,
Sun, moon, and stars forgot,
    Upward I fly;
Still all my song shall be,
Nearer, my God, to Thee,
    Nearer to Thee!

*Sarah F. Adams.*

## 193.

L. M. (6 lines.)     T. 96.

When gathering clouds around I view,
And days are dark, and friends are few,
On Him I lean, who, not in vain,
Experienc'd every human pain:
He sees my wants, allays my fears,
And counts and treasures up my tears.

PATIENCE AND TRUST.

2. If aught should tempt my soul to stray
From heavenly wisdom's narrow way,
To flee the good I would pursue,
Or do the sin I would not do;
Still He, who felt temptation's power,
Shall guard me in that dangerous hour.

3. When sorrowing o'er some stone I bend,
Which covers all that was a friend,
And from his hand, his voice, his smile,
Divides me for a little while;
My Saviour marks the tears I shed,
For Jesus wept o'er Lazarus dead.

4. And oh, when I have safely pass'd
Through every conflict but the last.
Still, Lord, unchanging watch beside
My dying bed, for Thou hast died;
Then point to realms of cloudless day,
And wipe the latest tear away.

Robert Grant.

11s.  **194.**  T. 39.

Begone, unbelief! for my Saviour is near,
And for my relief He will surely appear;
By prayer let me wrestle, and He will perform;
With Christ in the vessel I smile at the storm.

2. Tho' dark be my way, yet since He is my guide,
'Tis mine to obey, and 'tis His to provide;
Tho' cisterns be broken, and creatures all fail,
The word He hath spoken will surely prevail.

3. His love in time past me forbiddeth to think,
He'll leave me at last unrelieved to sink:
Each sweet Ebenezer I have in review,
Confirms His good pleasure to help me quite through.

PATIENCE AND TRUST.

4. Why should I complain then of want or distress,
Temptation or pain? for He told me no less;
The heirs of salvation, I know from His word,
Thro' much tribulation must follow their Lord.

5. How bitter the cup none can ever conceive,
Which Jesus drank up that poor sinners might live:
His way was much rougher and darker than mine;
Did Jesus thus suffer, and shall I repine?

6. Since all that I meet with shall work for my good,
The bitter is sweet and the medicine food;
Though painful at present, 'twill cease before long,
And then, O how pleasant the conqueror's song.
J. Newton.

## 195.

S. M.                                                      T. 14.

One prayer I have—all prayers in one—
   When I am wholly Thine;
Thy will, my God, Thy will be done,
   And let that will be mine.

2. All-wise, almighty, and all-good,
   In Thee I firmly trust;
Thy ways, unknown or understood,
   Are merciful and just.

3. May I remember that to Thee
   Whate'er I have I owe;
And back, in gratitude from me
   May all Thy bounties flow.

4. And though thy wisdom takes away,
   Shall I arraign Thy will?
No, let me bless Thy name, and say,
   "The Lord is gracious still."

5. A pilgrim through the earth I roam,
   Of nothing long possess'd,
And all must fail when I go home,
   For this is not my rest.
Montgomery.

## 196.

7s.   T. 11.

Poor and needy though I be,
God, my Maker, cares for me;
Gives me clothing, shelter, food,
Gives me all I have of good.

2. He will listen when I pray,
He is with me night and day,
When I sleep and when I wake,
Keeps me safe for Jesus' sake.

3. He who reigns above the sky
Once became as poor as I;
He whose blood for me was shed
Had not where to lay His head.

4. Though I labor here awhile,
He will bless me with His smile;
And when this short life is past,
I shall rest with Him at last.

## 197.

C. M.   T. 14.

We are not orphans on the earth,
  Though friends and parents die;
One Parent never bows to death,
  One Friend is ever nigh.

2. Even He who lit the stars of old,
  And filled the ocean broad,
Whose works and ways are manifold,
  Our Father is our God.

3. There comes no change upon His years,
  No failure to His hand;
His love will lighten all our cares,
  His law our steps command.

PATIENCE AND TRUST. 167

4. May He who for our sakes the gloom
   Of death's dark valley trod,
Bring us all safe at last to Him,
   Our Father and our God!

C. M.
## 198.
T. 14.

Father, whate'er of earthly bliss
   Thy sovereign will denies,
Accepted at Thy throne, let this
   Sincere petition rise:—

2. Give me a calm and thankful heart,
   From every murmur free;
The blessings of Thy grace impart,
   And let me live to Thee.

3. Let the sweet hope that Thou art mine,
   My life and death attend;
Thy presence through my journey shine,
   And crown my journey's end.
*Anna Steele.*

7s.
## 199.
T. 1L.

O how soft that bed must be,
Made in sickness, Lord, by Thee;
And that rest, how calm, how sweet,
Where Thou and the sufferer meet.

2. 'Twas the good Physician now,
Soothed thy cheek, and chafed thy brow,
Whispering, as He raised thy head—
"It is I, be not afraid."

3. God of glory, God of grace,
Hear from heaven, Thy dwelling-place,
Hear in mercy, and forgive,
Bid Thy child believe and live.

4. Bless me and I shall be blest,
Soothe me, and I shall have rest;
Fix my heart, my hopes, above;
Love me, Lord, for Thou art love.

S. M.

## 200.

T. 582 or 595.

"My times are in Thy hand!"
  My God, I wish them there;
My life, my friends, my soul, I leave
  Entirely to Thy care.

2. "My times are in Thy hand!"
    Whatever they may be,
  Pleasing or painful, dark or bright,
    As best may seem to Thee.

3. "My times are in Thy hand!"
    Why should I doubt or fear?
  My Father's love will never cause
    His child a needless tear.

4. "My times are in Thy hand!"
    Jesus, the Crucified!
  The hand my many sins have pierced,
    Is now my Guard and Guide.

5. "My times are in Thy hand!"
    Jesus, my Advocate;
  Nor shall Thine hand be raised in vain,
    For me to supplicate.

6. "My times are in Thy hand!"
    I'll always trust in Thee;
  Till I have left this weary land,
    And all Thy glory see.

## THE CHRISTIAN CHURCH, AND ITS ORDINANCES.

Matt. xviii. 20. Ephesians i. 22, 23.

8s. & 7s. Double.   **201.**   T. 167.

Glorious things of Thee are spoken,
  Zion, city of our God;
He whose word cannot be broken,
  Form'd thee for His own abode:
On the Rock of ages founded,
  What can shake thy sure repose?
With salvation's walls surrounded,
  Thou mayst smile at all thy foes.

2. Blest inhabitants of Zion,
  Wash'd in the Redeemer's blood!
Jesus, whom their souls rely on,
  Makes them kings and priests to God:
'Tis His love His people raises
  In His courts to reign as kings,
And as priests His solemn praises
  Each for a thank-offering brings.

3. Saviour, if of Zion's city
  I thro' grace a member am,
Let the world deride or pity,
  I will glory in Thy name;
Fading is the worldling's pleasure,
  All his boasted pomp and show;
Solid joy and lasting treasure
  None but Zion's children know.
                        J. Newton.

L. M.   **202.**   T. 22.

"As birds their infant brood protect,
And spread their wings to shelter them;"
Thus saith the Lord to his elect,
"So will I guard Jerusalem."

2. And what, then, is Jerusalem,
The darling object of His care?
What is its worth in God's esteem?
Who built it? who inhabits there?

3. Jehovah founded it in blood,
The blood of His incarnate Son;
There dwell the saints, once foes to God,
The sinners whom He calls His own.

4. Tho' foes on every side assail,
This city has a sure defence;
Against her they shall ne'er prevail,
While guarded by Omnipotence.

Cowper.

S. M.     **203.**     T. 595.

I love Thy kingdom Lord,
  The house of Thine abode,
The Church our blest Redeemer saved
  With His own precious blood.

2. I love Thy church, O God!
  Her walls before Thee stand,
Dear as the apple of Thine eye,
  And graven on Thy hand.

3. For her my tears shall fall,
  For her my prayers ascend;
To her my cares and toils be given,
  Till toils and cares shall end.

4. Beyond my highest joy
  I prize her heavenly ways,
Her sweet communion, solemn vows,
  Her hymns of love and praise.

5. Jesus, Thou Friend divine,
  Our Saviour, and our King,

Thy hand from every snare and foe
  Shall great deliverance bring.

6. Sure as Thy truth shall last,
  To Zion shall be given
The brightest glories earth can yield,
  And brighter bliss of heaven.

Dwight.

## 204.

C M.  T. 14.

Come, let us join our friends above,
  That have obtained the prize,
And on the eagle wings of love,
  To joys celestial rise.

2. Let saints below in concert sing
  With those to glory gone:
For all the servants of our king
  In heaven and earth are one.

3. One family, we dwell in Him,
  One church above, beneath,
Though now divided by the stream,
  The narrow stream of death.

4. One army of the living God,
  To His command we bow;
Part of the host have cross'd the flood,
  And part are crossing now.

5. Ten thousand to their endless home,
  This solemn moment fly;
And we are to the margin come,
  And we expect to die.

6. E'en now we join our hands
  With those that went before;
And greet the blood-besprinkled bands
  On the eternal shore.

## THE SACRAMENTS.

7. Oh! that we now might grasp our Guide!
Oh! that the word were given!
Come, Lord of Hosts, the waves divide,
And land us all in heaven!

C. Wesley.

## THE SACRAMENTS.

### 205.

C. M.            T. 14.

My Saviour God, my Sovereign Prince
  Reigns far above the skies;
But brings His graces down to sense,
  And helps my faith to rise.

2. My eyes and ears shall bless His name:
  They read and hear His word:
My touch and taste shall do the same,
  When they receive the Lord.

3. Baptismal water is designed
  To seal His cleansing grace;
While at His feast of bread and wine,
  He gives His saints a place.

4. But not the waters of a flood
  Can make my flesh so clean
As by His spirit and His blood
  He'll wash my soul from sin.

5. Not choicest meats, nor noblest wines,
  So much my heart refresh,
As when my faith goes through the signs,
  And feeds upon His flesh.

6. I love the Lord, who stoops so low,
  To give His word a seal:
But the rich grace His hands bestow,
  Exceeds the figures still.

Watts.

*Holy Baptism.*

Matt. xxviii. 19.

L. M. **206.** T. 22.

'Twas the commission of our Lord,
"Go, teach the nations, and baptize;"
The nations have received the word,
Since He ascended to the skies.

2. He sits upon the eternal hills,
With grace and pardon in His hands,
And sends His covenant with the seals,
To bless the distant Christian lands.

3. "Repent and be baptized," He saith,
"For the remission of your sins;"
And thus our sense assists our faith,
And shows us what the gospel means.

4. Our souls He washes in His blood,
As water makes the body clean;
And the good Spirit from our God
Descends like purifying rain.

5. Thus we engage ourselves to Thee,
And seal our covenant with the Lord;
O may the great eternal Three
In heaven our solemn vows record.

*The Holy Communion.*

Matt. xxvi. 26–28. 1 Cor. x. 16; xi. 24–26.

**207.** T. 107.

Lord Jesus, who before Thy passion,
Distress'd and sorrowful to death,
To us the fruits of Thy oblation
In Thy last supper didst bequeath;
Accept our praise, Thou bounteous Giver
Of life to every true believer.

2. As oft as we enjoy this blessing,
Each sacred token doth declare
Thy dying love all thoughts surpassing;
And while we Thee in memory bear
At each returning celebration,
We show Thy death for our salvation.

3. Assurance of our pardon sealed
Is in this sacrament renew'd;
The soul with peace and joy is filled,
With Thy atoning blood bedew'd;
That stream from all defilement cleanses,
And life abundantly dispenses.

4. That bond of love, that mystic union,
By which to Thee, our Head, we're join'd,
Is closer drawn at each communion;
By love inspir'd we know Thy mind,
And feeding on Thy death and merit,
Are render'd one with Thee in spirit.

5. Thy flesh to us a pledge is given,
That ev'n our flesh, corrupt and vile,
Shall from the dust be rais'd to heaven,
And with unfading glories smile,
And soul and body be forever
At home with Thee, our Lord and Saviour.
J. J. Rambach.

C. M. **208.** T. 14.

According to Thy gracious word,
  In meek humility,
This will I do, my dying Lord,
  I will remember Thee.

2. Thy body, broken for my sake,
  My bread from heaven shall be;
Thy testamental cup I take,
  And thus remember Thee.

3. Gethsemane, can I forget?
    Or there Thy conflict see,
Thine agony and bloody sweat,
    And not remember Thee?

4. When to the cross I turn mine eyes,
    And rest on Calvary,
O Lamb of God, my sacrifice!
    I must remember Thee:—

5. Remember Thee, and all Thy pains,
    And all Thy love to me;
Yea, while a breath, a pulse remains,
    Will I remember Thee.

6. And when these failing lips grow dumb,
    And mind and memory flee,
When Thou shalt in Thy kingdom come,
    Jesus, remember me.

J Montgomery.

C. M.  **209.**  T. 14.

Lord, at Thy table I behold
The wonders of Thy grace,
But most of all admire that I
Should find a welcome place.

2. What strange surprising grace is this
That one so lost has room!
Jesus my weary soul invites,
And freely bids me come.

3. Ye saints below, and hosts of heaven,
Join all your praising powers;
No theme is like redeeming love,
No Saviour is like ours.

Stennett.

## THE SANCTUARY AND THE LORD'S DAY.

Ps. cxviii 24.

S. M.
### 210.
T. 595 or 582.

Welcome, sweet day of rest,
 That saw the Lord arise;
Welcome to this reviving breast,
 And these rejoicing eyes!

2. The King himself comes near,
 And feasts His saints to day;
Here we may sit, and see Him here,
 And love, and praise, and pray.

3. One day amidst the place,
 Where my dear God hath been,
Is sweeter than ten thousand days
 Of pleasurable sin.

4. My willing soul would stay
 In such a frame as this,
And sit and sing herself away
 To everlasting bliss.

Watts.

C. M.
### 211.
T. 14

Blest is the work, my God and King,
 To praise Thy glorious name:
By day Thy wondrous grace to sing,
 By night Thy truth proclaim.

2. We hail Thy day of rest, O Lord,
 And seek Thy house of prayer,
To meet Thy saints, to hear Thy word,
 And all Thy works declare.

3. Though sensual hearts, unchang'd by grace,
 Such heavenly joys despise,
Teach us to love Thy dwelling-place,
 Thy day of rest to prize:

## THE LORD'S DAY.

4. Till, fix'd within Thy courts above,
   Far nobler songs we raise,
Where every heart is fill'd with love,
   And every mouth with praise.

*Watts.*

H. M. [Lischer.]
## 212.

Welcome, delightful morn!
   Thou day of sacred rest,
I hail Thy kind return;
   Lord, make these moments blest.
From low delights and trifling toys
I soar to reach immortal joys.

2. Now may the King descend,
      And fill His throne of grace;
   Thy sceptre, Lord, extend,
      While saints address Thy face;
   Let sinners feel Thy quickening word,
   And learn to know and fear the Lord.

3. Descend, celestial Dove,
      With all Thy quickening powers;
   Reveal a Saviour's love,
      And bless these sacred hours;
   Then shall my soul new life obtain,
   Nor Sabbaths be enjoy'd in vain.

*Hayward.*

L. M.
## 213.
T. 22.

This day belongs to God alone,
This day He chooses for His own;
And we must neither work nor play,
Because it is God's holy day.

2. 'Tis well to have one day in seven,
That we may learn the way to heaven;
Then let us spend it as we should,
In serving God and being good.

3. And every Sabbath should be passed,
   As if we knew it were our last;
   What would the dying sinner give
   To have one Sabbath more to live!

## 214.
C. M.      T. 14.

Come, let us join with one accord
  In hymns around the throne;
This is the day our risen Lord
  Hath made and called His own.

2. This is the day which God hath blest,
   The brightest of the seven;
Type of that everlasting rest
   The saints enjoy in heaven.

3. Then let us in His name sing on,
   And hasten to that day
When our Redeemer shall come down,
   And shadows pass away.

4. Not one, but all our days below
   Let us in hymns employ;
And in our Lord rejoicing go
   To His eternal joy.

## 215.
C. M.     T. 14.

This is the day the Lord hath made;
  He calls the hours His own;
Let heaven rejoice, let earth be glad,
  And praise surround His throne.

2. To-day He rose and left the dead,
   And Satan's empire fell;
To-day the saints His triumphs spread,
   And all His wonders tell.

3. Hosanna to the anointed King,
   To David's holy Son!
Help us, O Lord! descend and bring
   Salvation from Thy throne.

4. Blest be the Lord, who comes to men
   With messages of grace;
Who comes, in God His Father's name,
   To save our sinful race.

5. Hosanna in the highest strains
   The Church on earth can raise;
The highest heavens, in which He reigns,
   Shall give Him nobler praise.   Watts.

## 216.

S. M.  T. 595.

Lord of the worlds above,
   How pleasant and how fair
The dwellings of thy grace and love,
   Thy earthly temples are!

2. To Thy divine abode
   My longing heart aspires,
And pants to see the living God
   With ever warm desires.

3. To spend one sacred day,
   Where God and saints abide,
Affords the soul diviner joy
   Than thousand days beside.

4. Humbly to keep the door
   Where God, the Lord, resorts,—
A thousand times I love it more
   Than shine in splendid courts.

5. Thrice bless'd and happy he,
   Whose spirit humbly trusts
For each good gift alone in Thee,
   Jehovah, Lord of hosts.   Watts.

THE SANCTUARY AND THE LORD'S DAY.

L. M. **217.** T. 22.

Jesus, where'er Thy people meet,
There they behold Thy mercy-seat;
Where'er they seek Thee, Thou art found,
And every place is hallow'd ground.

2. For Thou, within no walls confin'd,
Inhabitest the humble mind;
Such ever bring Thee where they come,
And going, take Thee to their home.

3. Dear Shepherd of Thy chosen few,
Thy former mercies here renew;
Here to our waiting hearts proclaim
The sweetness of Thy saving name.

4. Here may we prove the power of prayer,
To strengthen faith, and sweeten care,
To teach our faint desires to rise,
And bring Thy cross before our eyes.

5. Behold, at Thy commanding word,
We stretch the curtain and the cord:
O rend the heavens and come down,
And make each rebel heart Thine own.    Cowper.

**218.** T. 97.

How sweet Thy dwellings, Lord, how fair;
What peace, what bliss inhabit there:
With ardent hope, with strong desire,
My heart, my flesh, to Thee aspire:
How oft I long Thy heavenly courts and Thee,
My Lord and God, the living God, to see.

2. One wish, with holy transport warm,
My heart hath form'd and still doth form:
One gift I ask, that to my end
Thine hallow'd house I may attend;
There may I joyful find a safe abode,
There may I view the beauty of my God.

## TIME AND ETERNITY.

Prov. xxvii. 1.   Eccles. xii. 1.   2 Cor. vi. 2.

C. M.
### 219.
T. 14.

Time! what an empty vapor 'tis!
  And days, how swift they are!
Swift as an Indian arrow flies,
  Or like a shooting star.

2. The present moments just appear,
  Then glide away in haste;
That we can never say, "they're here,"
  But only say, "they're past."

3. Our life is ever on the wing,
  And death is ever nigh!
The moment when our lives begin,
  We all begin to die.

4. Yet, mighty God! our fleeting days
  Thy lasting favors share;
Yet, with the bounties of Thy grace,
  Thou load'st the rolling year.

5. 'Tis sovereign mercy finds us food,
  And we are cloth'd with love;
While grace stands pointing out the road
  That leads our souls above.

Watts.

C. M.
### 220.
T. 14.

Thee we adore, Eternal Name!
  And humbly own to Thee;
How feeble is our mortal frame,
  What dying worms are we!

2. Our wasting lives grow shorter still,
  As months and days increase;
And every beating pulse we tell,
  Leaves but the number less.

TIME AND ETERNITY.

3. The year rolls round, and steals away
  The breath that first it gave;
Whate'er we do, where'er we be,
  We're traveling to the grave.

4. Dangers stand thick through all the ground,
  To push us to the tomb;
And fierce diseases wait around,
  To hurry mortals home.

5. Great God! on what a slender thread
  Hang everlasting things!
Th' eternal state of all the dead
  Upon life's feeble strings.

6. Infinite joy, or endless woe,
  Attends on every breath;
And yet how unconcerned we go,
  Upon the brink of death!
*Watts.*

L. M.
## 221.
T. 22.

Ere mountains reared their forms sublime,
  Or heaven and earth in order stood,
Before the birth of ancient time,
  From everlasting Thou art God.

2. A thousand ages in their flight,
  With Thee are as a fleeting day;
Past, present, future, to Thy sight
  At once their various scenes display.

3. But our brief life's a shadowy dream,
  A passing thought that soon is o'er,
That fades with morning's earliest beam,
  And fills the musing mind no more.

4. To us, O Lord, the wisdom give,
  Each passing moment so to spend,
That we at length with Thee may live
  Where life and bliss shall never end.

TIME AND ETERNITY.

## 222.

8s. & 7s.*  T. 16.

My days are gliding swiftly by,
  And I, a pilgrim stranger,
Would not detain them as they fly,—
  Those hours of toil and danger.

2. We'll gird our loins, companions dear,
  Our heavenly home discerning;
Our absent Lord has left us word,
  Let every lamp be burning.

3. Should coming days be cold and dark,
  We need not cease our singing;
That perfect rest nought can molest
  Where golden harps are ringing.

4. Let sorrow's rudest tempest blow,
  Each chord on earth to sever;
Our King says, come, and there's our home,
  For ever, oh! for ever!

CHORUS.

For, oh! we stand on Jordan's strand,
  Our friends are passing over,
And, just before, the shining shore
  We may almost discover.

Nelson.

## 223.

6s.†

One sweetly solemn thought
  Comes to me o'er and o'er:
I'm nearer my home to-day
  Than I've ever been before.

2. Nearer my Father's house,
  Where the many mansions be;
Nearer the great white throne,
  Nearer the jasper sea.

* P. S. S. Coll., p. 87.   † Fresh Laurels, p. 69.

TIME AND ETERNITY.

3. Nearer the bound of life,
   Where we lay our burdens down,
Nearer leaving the cross,
   Nearer wearing the crown.

4. But lying darkly between,
   Winding down through the night,
Is that dim and unknown stream
   Which leads at last to light.

5. Father, perfect my trust,
   Strengthen my feeble faith,
Let me feel as if I trod
   The shore of the river death.

6. For even now my feet
   May stand upon its brink;
I may be nearer my home,
   Nearer now, than I think.  Phœbe Cary.

7s. & 6s. [Amsterdam.] **224.**

Rise, my soul, and stretch thy wings,
Thy better portion trace;
Rise from transitory things
Toward heaven, thy native place:
Sun, and moon, and stars decay,
Time shall soon this earth remove,
Rise, my soul, and haste away
To seats prepar'd above.

2. Rivers to the ocean run,
Nor stay in all their course;
Fire ascending, seeks the sun;
Both speed them to their source:
So, a soul that's born of God,
Pants to view His glorious face;
Upward tends to His abode,
To rest in His embrace.

TIME AND ETERNITY.

3. Cease, ye pilgrims, cease to mourn,
Press onward to the prize;
Soon our Saviour will return,
Triumphant in the skies:
Yet a season, and we know
Happy entrance will be giv'n;
All our sorrows left below,
And earth exchang'd for heaven.

Seagrave.

C. M.    **225.**    T. 14.

Oh, 'tis a folly and a crime
  To put religion by;
For now is the accepted time,
  To-morrow we may die.

2. Our hearts grow harder every day,
  And more depraved the mind;
The longer we neglect to pray,
  The less we feel inclined.

3. Yet sinners trifle, young and old,
  Until the dying day;
Then they would give a world of gold
  To have an hour to pray.

4. Oh, then, lest we should perish thus,
  We would no longer wait;
For time will soon be past with us,
  And death will fix our state.

C. M.    **226.**    T. 14.

Remember thy Creator now,
  In these thy youthful days;
He will accept thine earliest vow;
  He loves thine earliest praise.

2. Remember thy Creator now,
   Seek Him while He is near;
For evil days will come, when thou
   Shalt find no comfort here.

3. Remember thy Creator now,
   His willing servant be;
Then, when thy head in death shall bow,
   He will remember thee.

4. Almighty God, our hearts incline
   Thy heavenly voice to hear;
Let all our future days be Thine,
   Devoted to Thy fear.

C. M.                **227.**                T. 14.

Beneath our feet and o'er our head
   Is equal warning given:
Beneath us lie the countless dead,
   Above us is the heaven!

2. Death rides on every passing breeze,
   And lurks in every flower;
Each season has its own disease,
   Its peril every hour!

3. Our eyes have seen the rosy light
   Of youth's soft cheek decay;
And fate descend in sudden night
   On manhood's middle day.

4. Our eyes have seen the steps of age
   Halt feebly to the tomb;
And yet shall earth our hearts engage,
   And dreams of days to come?

5. Then, mortal, turn! thy danger know;
   Where'er thy foot can tread,
The earth rings hollow from below,
   And warns thee of her dead!

6. Turn, mortal, turn! thy soul apply
   To truths divinely given:
The dead, who underneath thee lie,
   Shall live for hell or heaven!

Heber.

## 228.

7s.*   T. 11 or 205.

Little travelers Zion-ward,
   Each one entering into rest,
In the kingdom of your Lord,
   In the mansions of the blest,
There to welcome Jesus waits,
   Gives the crowns His followers win:
Lift your heads, ye golden gates,
   Let the little travelers in.

2. Who are those whose little feet,
   Pacing life's dark journey through,
Now have reach'd that heavenly seat
   They had ever kept in view?
"I, from Greenland's frozen land;"
   "I, from India's sultry plain;"
"I, from Afric's barren sand;"
   "I, from islands of the main."

3. "All our earthly journey past,
   Every tear and pain gone by,
Here together met at last
   At the portal of the sky!"
Each the welcome "Come" awaits,
   Conquerors over death and sin:
Lift your heads, ye golden gates,
   Let the little travelers in.

* P. S. S. Coll., p. 59.

TIME AND ETERNITY.

P. M.*

## 229.

We are out on an ocean sailing
  Homeward bound, we smoothly glide;
We are out on an ocean sailing
  To a home beyond the tide.

CHORUS.
All the storms will soon be over,
Then we'll anchor in the harbor;
We are out on an ocean, sailing
  To a home beyond the tide.

2. Millions now are safely landed
  Over on the golden shore;
Millions now are on their journey,
  Yet there's room for millions more.

CHORUS.
All the storms, &c.

3. When we all are safely anchor'd,
  We will shout our journey o'er,
We will walk about the city,
  And will sing for evermore.

CHORUS.
All the storms, &c.

C. M.

## 230.

T. 14.

There is a time,—we know not when,—
  A point,—we know not where,—
Which marks the destiny of men
  To glory or despair.

2. There is a line, by us unseen,
  That crosses every path—
The hidden boundary between
  God's patience and His wrath.

\* Golden Chain, p. 87.

3. How far may we go on in sin?
   How long will God forbear?
Where does hope end, and where begin
   The confines of despair?

4. An answer from the skies is sent:
   "Ye who from God depart,
While it is called to-day, *repent*,
   And harden not your heart."

J. A. Alexander.

## DEATH, RESURRECTION AND JUDGMENT.

### 231.

L. M.  T. 22.

The moment comes, the only one
   Of all my time to be foretold;
Though when, and where, and how, can none
   Of all the race of man unfold.

2. That moment comes, when strength must fail,
   When, health and hope and comfort flown,
I must go down into the vale
   And shade of death, with Thee alone.

3. Then, when th' undying spirit lands
   Where flesh and blood have never trod,
And in the unveil'd presence stands
   Of Thee, my Saviour and my God,

4. Be mine eternal portion this,
   Since Thou wert always here with me,
That I may view Thy face in bliss,
   And be for evermore with Thee.

Montgomery.

S. M.

## 232.

T. 582.

And am I born to die?
  To lay this body down?
And must my trembling spirit fly
  Into a world unknown?

2. Waked by the trumpet's sound,
  I from the grave must rise;
And see the Judge, with glory crowned,
  And see the flaming skies.

3. How shall I leave my tomb?
  With triumph or regret?
A fearful, or a joyful doom—
  A curse, or blessing—meet?

4. I must from God be driven,
  Or with my Saviour dwell;
Must come at his command, to heaven;
  Or else depart—to hell.

5. O Thou, that wouldst not have
  One wretched sinner die,—
Who diedst thyself, my soul to save
  From endless misery,—

6. Show me the way to shun
  Thy dreadful wrath, severe;
That, when Thou comest on Thy throne,
  I may with joy appear.

C. M.

## 233.

T. 14.

Teach me the measure of my days,
  Thou maker of my frame!
I would survey life's narrow space,
  And learn how frail I am.

2. A span is all that we can boast,
  A fleeting hour of time:

Man is but vanity and dust,
  In all his flow'r and prime.

3. See the vain race of mortals move,
  Like shadows o'er the plain:
They rage and strive, desire and love,
  But all their noise is vain.

4. Some walk in honor's gaudy show;
  Some dig for golden ore;
The toil for heirs, they know not who,
  And straight are seen no more.

5. What should I wish or wait for, then,
  From creatures, earth and dust?
They make our expectations vain,
  And disappoint our trust.

6. Now I resign my earthly hope,
  My fond desires recall;
I give my mortal int'rest up,
  And make my God my all. *Watts.*

11s.* **234.** T. 39.

I would not live alway; I ask not to stay,
Where storm after storm rises dark o'er the way;
The few lucid mornings that dawn on us here,
Are enough for life's woes, full enough for its cheer.

2. I would not live alway, thus fetter'd by sin;
Temptation without, and corruption within:
E'en the rapture of pardon is mingled with fears,
And the cup of thanksgiving with penitent tears.

3. I would not live alway; no—welcome the tomb,
Since Jesus has lain there, I dread not its gloom;
There, sweet be my rest, till He bid me arise
To hail Him in triumph descending the skies.

* P. S. S. Coll., p. 186.

4. Who, who would live alway, away from his God;
Away from yon heaven, that blissful abode,
Where the rivers of pleasure flow o'er the bright plains,
And the noontide of glory eternally reigns:—

5. Where the saints of all ages in harmony meet,
Their Saviour and brethren transported to greet;
While the anthems of rapture unceasingly roll,
And the smile of the Lord is the feast of the soul.

Muhlenberg.

*Death of a Teacher.*

L. M.  **235.**  T. 22.

Lord, thou hast called Thy servant home:
He now has yielded up his trust;
*His* body, in the silent tomb,
Must moulder with its kindred dust.

2. No more shall *he*, with cheerful feet,
Tread in the paths of duty now;
No more *his* precious charge shall meet,
Nor worship in Thy courts below.

3. Earth claims *his* earthly part again;
*His* spirit mounts to yonder skies;
And, with the loudest of the train
That harp their Saviour's praises, vies.

4. We bless Thy name, Thou King of Saints,
That Thou such bright rewards hast given;
Oh, when our wearied spirit faints,
Refresh us with a glimpse of heaven.

5. And when the appointed hour is come,
That we this earthly scene must leave,
May angel-guards conduct us home,
The crown of glory to receive.

*Death of a Scholar.*

C. M.  **236.**  T. 14.

Death has been here, and borne away
  A scholar from our side:
Just in the morning of *his* day,
  As young as we, *he* died.

2. Not long ago, *he* filled *his* place,
  And sat with us to learn;
But *he* has run *his* mortal race,
  And never can return.

3. Perhaps our time may be as short,
  Our days may fly as fast;
O Lord, impress the solemn thought,
  That this may be our last.

4. We cannot tell who next may fall
  Beneath Thy chastening rod;
One must be first; oh, may we all
  Prepare to meet our God!

5. All needful help is Thine to give;
  To Thee our souls apply,
For grace to teach us how to live,
  And make us fit to die.


8s. & 7s.  **237.**  T. 167.

Happy soul! thy days are ended,
  All thy mourning days below;
Go, by angel guards attended,
  To the sight of Jesus go
Waiting to receive thy spirit,
  Lo! the Saviour stands above;
Shows the purchase of His merit,
  Reaches out the crown of love.

2. Struggle through thy latest passion
   To thy dear Redeemer's breast,
To His uttermost salvation,
   To His everlasting rest;
For the joy He sets before thee,
   Bear a momentary pain;
Die, to live a life of glory;
   Suffer, with thy Lord to reign.

*C. Wesley.*

L. M.
## 238.
T. 22.

Why should we start and fear to die?
What timorous worms we mortals are!
Death is the gate to endless joy,
And yet we dread to enter there.

2. The pains, the groans, the dying strife,
Fright our approaching souls away;
And we shrink back again to life,
Fond of our prison and our clay.

3. O, if my Lord would come and meet,
My soul would stretch her wings in haste,
Fly fearless through death's iron gate,
Nor feel the terrors as she passed.

4. Jesus can make a dying bed
Feel soft as downy pillows are,
While on His breast I lean my head,
And breathe my life out sweetly there.

*Watts.*

L. M.
## 239.
T. 22.

Dearest of names, our Lord, our King!
Jesus, Thy praise we humbly sing:
In cheerful songs we'll spend our breath,
And in Thee triumph over death.

2. Death is no more among our foes,
Since Christ, the mighty Conqueror, rose;
Both power and sting the Saviour broke;
He died, and gave the finished stroke.

3. Saints die, and we should gently weep;
Sweetly in Jesus' arms they sleep;
Far from this world of sin and woe,
Nor sin, nor pain, nor grief, they know.

4. Death no terrific foe appears,
An angel's lovely form he wears;
A friendly messenger he proves
To every soul whom Jesus loves.

5. Death is a sleep; and oh! how sweet
To souls prepared its stroke to meet!
Their dying beds, their graves are blest,
For all to them is peace and rest.

6. Their bodies sleep; their souls take wing,
Uprise to Heaven, and there they sing
With joy before the Saviour's face,
Triumphant in victorious grace.

7. Soon shall the earth's remotest bound
Feel the Archangel's trumpet sound;
Then shall the grave's dark cavern shake,
And joyful all the saints shall wake.

8. Bodies and souls shall then unite,
Arrayed in glory, strong and bright;
And all His saints will Jesus bring
His face to see, His love to sing.

9. O may I live, with Jesus nigh,
And sleep in Jesus when I die!
Then, joyful, when from death I wake,
I shall eternal bliss partake.

*Medley.*

## 240.

T. 83.

Christ, my rock, my sure defence,
Jesus, my Redeemer, liveth!
O what pleasing hopes from thence
My believing heart deriveth!
Else death's long and gloomy night
Would my guilty soul affright.

2. Christ is risen from the dead,
"Thou shalt rise too," saith my Saviour;
Of what should I be afraid?
I with Him shall live forever;
Can the Head forsake His limb,
And not draw me unto Him?—

3. No, my soul He cannot leave,
This, this is my consolation;
And my body in the grave
Rests in hope and expectation,
That this mortal flesh shall see
Incorruptibility.

4. Let us raise our minds above
This world's lusts, vain, transitory,
Cleave to Him e'vn here in love,
Whom we hope to see in glory;
May our minds tend constantly
Where we ever wish to be.

Louisa of Brandenburg.

## 241.

C. M.          T. 590.

My faith shall triumph o'er the grave,
And trample on the tombs;
My Jesus, my Redeemer lives,
My God, my Saviour comes:
Ere long I know He shall appear
In power and glory great;
And death, the last of all His foes,
Lie vanquish'd at His feet.

2. Then, tho' the worms my flesh devour,
And make my corpse their prey,
I know I shall arise with power,
On the last judgment-day;
When God shall stand upon the earth,
Him these mine eyes shall see,
My flesh shall feel a second birth,
And ever with Him be.

3. Then His own hand shall wipe the tears,
From every weeping eye;
And pains, and groans, and griefs, and fears,
Shall cease eternally:
How long, dear Saviour, O how long,
Shall this bright hour delay?
Oh, hasten Thy appearance, Lord,
And bring the welcome day.

Watts.

L. M.    **242.**    T. 22.

Unveil thy bosom, faithful tomb;
*Take this new treasure to thy trust,
And give these sacred relics room
To slumber in the silent dust.

2. Nor pain, nor grief, nor anxious fear,
Invade thy bounds; no mortal woes
Can reach the peaceful sleeper here,
While angels watch the soft repose.

3. So Jesus slept; God's dying Son
Passed though the grave, and blest the bed:
Rest here, blest saint, till from His throne
The morning break, and pierce the shade.

4. Break from His throne, illustrious morn;
Attend, O earth, His sovereign word;
Restore thy trust; a glorious form
Shall then arise to meet the Lord.

Watts.

DEATH, RESURRECTION

C. M.
### 243.
T. 14.

When rising from the bed of death,
  O'erwhelm'd with guilt and fear,
I see my Maker face to face,
  Oh, how shall I appear?

2. If yet while pardon may be found,
  Thy mercy I've not sought,
My heart with inward horror shrinks,
  And trembles at the thought,—

3. That Thou, O Lord, wilt stand disclos'd
  In majesty severe,
And sit in judgment on my soul:
  How then shall I appear?

4. But Thou declarest in Thy word,
  That sinners who to Thee,
While here they live, repenting turn,
  Shall live eternally.

5. Grant then, that I may favor'd be,
  Full pardon to obtain,
Since Jesus Christ, to save my soul,
  Upon the cross was slain.

*Addison.*

S. M.
### 244.
T. 582.

A dread and solemn hour
  To us is drawing near;
When we before the throne of God
  All present shall appear.

2. What answer shall we give,
  When God himself demands
The uses of such times as these,
  In judgment at our hands?

3. And must we then confess
   That all was spent in vain,—
The seasons that were once our own,
   But cannot be again?

4. This will be woe indeed:
   To regions of despair,
Our own neglect will sink us down,
   To mourn for ever there.

## 245.

8s. 7s. & 4s.  T. 585.

Day of judgment! day of wonders!
Hark, the trumpet's awful sound,
Louder than a thousand thunders,
Shakes the vast creation round:
How the summons :‖:
Will the sinner's heart confound!

2. See the Judge our nature wearing,
Cloth'd in majesty divine;
Ye who love the Lord's appearing,
Then shall say, "This God is mine:"
Gracious Saviour, :‖:
Own me on that day as Thine.

3. At His call the dead awaken,
Rise to life from earth and sea;
All the powers of nature shaken,
At His call prepare to flee:
Careless sinner, :‖:
What will then become of thee?

4. Then to all who have confessed,
Lov'd and serv'd the Lord below,
He will say, "Come near, ye blessed,
See the kingdom I bestow:
You for ever :‖:
Shall my love and glory know."

## HEAVEN.

5. Under sorrows and reproaches
May this thought our courage raise,
Swiftly God's great day approaches;
Sighs will then be chang'd to praise:
We shall triumph :‖:
When the world is in a blaze.

J. Newton.

---

### HEAVEN.
Ps. xvi. 11. Hebr. xi. 16. John xiv. 2. Rev. xxi. 1-4.

C. M. **246.** T. 14.

There is a house not made with hands,
Eternal, and above;
And here my spirit waiting stands,
Till it shall hence remove.

2. My Saviour by His saving grace
Prepareth me for heaven;
And, as an earnest of the place,
Hath His own spirit giv'n.

3. We walk by faith of joys to come,
Faith lives upon His word;
But while the body is our home,
We're absent from the Lord.

4. 'Tis pleasant to believe Thy grace,
But we would rather see;
We would be absent from the flesh,
And present, Lord, with Thee.

Watts.

C. M. **247.** T. 14.

There is a land of pure delight
Where saints immortal reign;
Infinite day excludes the night,
And pleasures banish pain.

2. There everlasting spring abides,
   And never-withering flowers,
Death, like a narrow sea, divides
   This heavenly land from ours.

3. Sweet fields, beyond the swelling flood,
   Stand dressed in living green;
So to the Jews old Canaan stood,
   While Jordan rolled between.

4. Could we but climb where Moses stood,
   And view the landscape o'er,
Not Jordan's stream, nor death's cold flood
   Should fright us from the shore.

                              Watts.

## 248.

6s. & 4s.*

There is a happy land,
   Far, far away,—
Where saints in glory stand,
   Bright, bright as day:
Oh, how they sweetly sing,—
"Worthy is our Saviour King;
Loud let His praises ring
   Praise, praise for aye."

2. Come to this happy land,
   Come, come away;
Why will ye doubting stand?
   Why still delay?
Oh, we shall happy be,
When, from sin and sorrow free,
Lord, we shall live with Thee,
   Blest, blest for aye.

3. Bright, in that happy land,
   Beams every eye;
Kept by a Father's hand,
   Love cannot die.

    \* Happy Voices, No. 1.

HEAVEN.

Oh, then to glory run;
Be a crown and kingdom won;
And bright above the sun,
  We reign for aye.

P. M.*  **249.**

I'm a pilgrim and I'm a stranger;
I can tarry, I can tarry but a night.
Do not detain me, for I am going
To where the fountains are ever flowing.
  I'm a pilgrim, &c.

2. There the glory is ever shining:
I am longing, I am longing for the sight.
Here in this country, so dark and dreary,
I have been wandering forlorn and weary.
  I'm a pilgrim, &c.

3. There's the city to which I journey;
My Redeemer, my Redeemer is its light;
There is no sorrow, nor any sighing,
There is no sin there nor any dying.
  I'm a pilgrim, &c.

C. M.  **250.**  T. 14.

Jerusalem, my happy home!
  Name ever dear to me!
When shall my labors have an end,
  In joy, and peace, and thee?

2. When shall these eyes thy heaven-built walls
  And pearly gates behold?
Thy bulwarks, with salvation strong,
  And streets of shining gold?

\* Happy Voices, No. 209.

3. There happier bowers than Eden's bloom,
   Nor sin nor sorrow know;
Bless'd seats! through rude and stormy scenes
   I onward press to you.

4. Why should I shrink from pain and woe,
   And feel at death dismay?
I've Canaan's goodly land in view,
   And realms of endless day.

5. Apostles, martyrs, prophets there
   Around my Saviour stand;
And soon my friends in Christ below,
   Will join the glorious band.

6. Jerusalem, my happy home!
   My soul still pants for thee;
Then shall my labors have an end,
   When I thy joys shall see.

C. M.  **251.**  T. 14.

Come, Lord, and warm each languid heart,
   Inspire each lifeless tongue:
And let the joys of heaven impart
   Their influence to our song.

2. Sorrow, and pain, and every care,
   And discord, there shall cease;
And perfect joy and love sincere,
   Adorn the realms of peace.

3. The soul, from sin for ever free,
   Shall mourn its power no more;
But, cloth'd in spotless purity,
   Redeeming love adore.

Steele.

HEAVEN.

C. M.
## 252.
T. 14.

O mother dear, Jerusalem,
　When shall I come to thee?
When shall my sorrows have an end?
　Thy joys when shall I see?

2. O happy harbor of God's saints!
　O sweet and pleasant soil!
In thee no sorrow can be found,
　Nor grief, nor care, nor toil.

3. No murky cloud o'ershadows thee,
　Nor gloom, nor darksome night;
But every soul shines as the sun,
　For God himself gives light.

4. Thy walls are made of precious stone,
　Thy bulwarks diamond-square,
Thy gates are all orient pearl—
　O God! if I were there!

5. O my sweet home, Jerusalem!
　Thy joys when shall I see?—
The King that sitteth on thy throne
　In His felicity?

6. Thy gardens and thy goodly walks
　Continually are green,
Where grow such sweet and pleasant flowers
　As no where else are seen.

7. Right through thy streets with silver sound
　The flood of life doth flow;
And on the banks on either side,
　The trees of life do grow.

8. Those trees each month yield ripened fruit;
　For evermore they spring,
And all the nations of the earth
　To thee their honors bring.

HEAVEN.

9. O mother dear, Jerusalem!
   When shall I come to thee?
When shall my sorrows have an end?
   Thy joys when shall I see?              Quarles.

C. M.                **253.**                    T. 14.

On Jordan's stormy banks I stand,
   And cast a wishful eye
To Canaan's fair and happy land,
   Where my possessions lie.

2. O the transporting, rapturous scene,
     That rises to my sight!
   Sweet fields arrayed in living green,
     And rivers of delight!

3. O'er all those wide extended plains
     Shines one eternal day;
   There God, the Sun, for ever reigns,
     And scatters night away.

4. No chilling winds, no poisonous breath,
     Can reach that healthful shore:
   Sickness and sorrow, pain and death,
     Are felt and feared no more.

5. When shall I reach that happy place,
     And be for ever blest?
   When shall I see my Father's face,
     And in His bosom rest?
                                          Stennett.

P. M.*              **254.**

Boys—Whither, pilgrims, are you going,
         Going each with staff in hand?
Girls.—We are going on a journey,
         Going at our King's command;

\* Golden Chain, p. 78.

HEAVEN.

All.—Over plains, and hills, and valleys,
We are going to His palace,
We are going to His palace,
Going to the better land.

Boys.—2. Fear ye not the way so lonely,
You, a little, feeble band?
Girls.—No, for friends unseen are near us,
Holy angels round us stand:
All.—Christ, our leader, walks beside us,
He will guard, and He will guide us,
He will guard, and He will guide us,
Going to that better land.

Boys.—3. Tell me, pilgrims, what you hope for,
In that far-off, better land?
Girls.—Spotless robes and crowns of glory,
From a Saviour's loving hand;
All.—We shall drink of life's clear river,
We shall dwell with God for ever,
We shall dwell with God for ever,
In that bright, that better land.

Boys.—4. Pilgrims, may we travel with you,
To that bright and better land?
Girls.—Come and welcome, come and welcome,
Welcome to our pilgrim band.
All.—Come, oh come! and do not leave us,
Christ is waiting to receive us,
Christ is waiting to receive us,
In that bright, that better land.

## 255.

10s.*

Joyfully, joyfully onward I move,
Bound for the land of bright spirits above;
Angelic choristers sing as I come,
"Joyfully, joyfully haste to thy home."

* Happy Voices, No. 211.

## HEAVEN.

Soon, with my pilgrimage ended below,
Home to that land of delight will I go;
Pilgrim and stranger no more shall I roam,
Joyfully, joyfully resting at home.

2. Friends fondly cherished have pass'd on before;
Waiting, they watch me approaching the shore,
Singing, to cheer me through death's chilling gloom,
"Joyfully, joyfully haste to thy home."
Sounds of sweet melody fall on my ear;
Harps of the blessed, your voices I hear!
Rings with the harmony heaven's high dome,
"Joyfully, joyfully haste to thy home."

3. Death, with thy weapons of war lay me low;
Strike, king of terrors, I fear not thy blow;
Jesus has broken the bars of the tomb;
Joyfully, joyfully will I go home.
Bright will the morn of eternity dawn;
Death shall be banish'd, his sceptre be gone:
Joyfully then shall I witness his doom;
Joyfully, joyfully, safely at home.

W. Hunter.

S. M.

## 256.

T. 582.

"For ever with the Lord!"
 Amen, so let it be;
Life from the dead is in that word,
 'T is immortality.

2. Here in the body pent,
 Absent from him I roam,
Yet nightly pitch my moving tent
 A day's march nearer home.

3. "For ever with the Lord!"
 Father, if 'tis thy will,
The promise of that faithful word
 E'en now to me fulfill.

4. Be Thou at my right hand,
   Then I can never fail;
Uphold Thou me, and I shall stand;
   Fight, and I must prevail.

5. So, when my latest breath
   Shall rend this vail in twain,
By death I shall escape from death,
   And life eternal gain.

5. Knowing as I am known,
   How shall I love that word,
And oft repeat before Thy throne:
   "For ever with the Lord!"

*Montgomery.*

## 257.

6s.*

We speak of the realms of the blest,
   Of that country so bright and so fair;
And oft are its glories confess'd;
   But what must it be to be there?
We speak of its pathways of gold,
   Of its walls deck'd with jewels so rare,
Of its wonders and pleasures untold.
   But what must it be to be there?

2. We speak of its freedom from sin,
   From sorrow, temptation and care,
From trials without and within;
   But what must it be to be there?
We speak of its service of love,
   Of the robes which the glorified wear,
Of the church of the first-born above;
   But what must it be to be there?

3. Do thou, Lord, midst gladness or woe,
   Still for heaven our spirits prepare,
And shortly we also shall know,
   And feel what it is to be there.

* Happy Voices, No. 206.

HEAVEN.

Then anthems of praise we will sing,
　When safe in that heavenly rest,
To Jesus, our Saviour and King,
　Who reigns in those realms of the blest.
　　　　　　　　　　　　　　　Wilson.

7s. Double.　　　**258.**　　　T. 205.

Who are these in bright array,
　This innumerable throng,
Round the altar, night and day,
　Hymning one triumphant song?
"Worthy is the Lamb once slain,
　Blessing, honor, glory, power,
Wisdom, riches, to obtain,
　New dominion every hour."

2. These through fiery trials trod,
　These from great afflictions came;
Now before the throne of God,
　Seal'd with His almighty name,
Clad in raiment pure and white,
　Victor-palms in every hand,
Through their dear Redeemer's might,
　More than conquerors they stand.

3. Hunger, thirst, disease, unknown,
　On immortal fruits they feed;
Them, the Lamb amidst the throne,
　Shall to living fountains lead:
Joy and gladness banish sighs,
　Perfect love dispels all fears,
And for ever from their eyes,
　God shall wipe away the tears.
　　　　　　　　　　　　　　Montgomery.

7s.　　　**259.**　　　T. 1L.

Palms of glory, raiment bright,
　Crowns that never fade away,
Gird and deck the saints in light;
　Priests, and kings, and conquerors, they.

14

HEAVEN.

2. Yet the conquerors bring their palms
   To the Lamb amid the throne;
And proclaim, in joyful psalms,
   Victory through His cross alone.

3. Kings for harps their crowns resign,
   Crying, as they strike the chords—
"Take the kingdom; it is Thine,
   King of kings, and Lord of lords."

4. Round the altar priests confess,
   If their robes are white as snow,
'Twas their Saviour's righteousness,
   And His blood, that made them so.

5. Who are these? On earth they dwelt,
   Sinners once of Adam's race;
Guilt, and fear, and suffering felt,
   But were saved by sovereign grace.

6. They were mortal, too, like us;
   Ah! when we, like them, shall die,
May our souls, translated thus,
   Triumph, reign, and shine, on high!
                                    Montgomery.

6s. & 4s.*  **260.**

I'm but a traveler here,
   Heaven is my home;
Earth is a desert drear,
   Heaven is my home:
Danger and sorrow stand
Round me on every hand,
Heaven is my fatherland,
   Heaven is my home.

2. What though the tempest rage,
   Heaven is my home;

* Happy Voices, No. 184.

Short is my pilgrimage,
  Heaven is my home:
Time's cold and wintry blast
Soon will be overpast,
I shall reach home at last,
  Heaven is my home.

3. There, at my Saviour's side,
  Heaven is my home;
I shall be glorified,
  Heaven is my home:
There are the good and bless'd,
Those I love most and best,
There, too, I soon shall rest,
  Heaven is my home.

C. M.*
## 261.
T. 14.

Around the throne of God in heaven,
  Thousands of children stand;
Children whose sins are all forgiven,
  A holy, happy band.
    [Singing, "Glory, glory,
    Glory be to God on high."]

2. In flowing robes of spotless white,
  See every one array'd;
Dwelling in everlasting light,
  And joys that never fade.
    [Singing, &c.]

3. What brought them to that world above?
  That heaven so bright and fair,
Where all is peace, and joy, and love;
  How came those children there?
    [Singing, &c.]

4. Because the Saviour shed His blood,
  To wash away their sin:

* Happy Voices, No. 11.

HEAVEN.

Bathed in that pure and precious flood,
  Behold them white and clean!
    [Singing, &c.]

5. On earth they sought the Saviour's grace,
  On earth they loved His name;
So now they see His blessed face,
  And stand before the Lamb.
    [Singing, &c.]

C. M.   **262.**   T. 14.

Happy the children who are gone
  To Jesus Christ in peace,
Who stand around His glorious throne,
  Clad in His righteousness.

2. The Saviour, whom they lov'd when here,
  Hath wip'd their tears away;
They never more can grieve, or fear,
  Or sin, or go astray.

3. In ceaseless happiness they view
  Our Saviour's smiling face;
That face once marr'd, in which below
  Men saw no comeliness.

4. Methinks I hear them joyful sing,
  ('Ten thousands do the same),
"Salvation to the immortal King,
  To God and to the Lamb."

5. O that I may so favor'd be;
  With them above to join:
O that, like them, I Christ may see,
  And He be ever mine.

6. Grant me but this, Thou great High-priest;
  And when I'm here no more,
Convey me home to endless rest,
  Where Thou art gone before.
                              Cennick.

## 263.

7s. & 6s.*

I want to be an angel,
  And with the angels stand,
A crown upon my forehead,
  A harp within my hand.
There, right before my Saviour,
  So glorious and so bright,
I'd make the sweetest music,
  And praise Him day and night.

2. I never should be weary,
  Nor ever shed a tear,
Nor ever know a sorrow,
  Nor ever feel a fear;
But blessed, pure and holy,
  I'd dwell in Jesus' sight,
And with ten thousand thousands
  Praise Him both day and night.

3. I know I'm weak and sinful,
  But Jesus will forgive,
For many little children
  Have gone to heaven to live.
Dear Saviour, when I languish,
  And lay me down to die,
Oh, send a shining angel
  To bear me to the sky.

4. Oh, there I'll be an angel,
  And with the angels stand,
A crown upon my forehead,
  A harp within my hand;
And there before my Saviour,
  So glorious and so bright,
I'll join the heavenly music,
  And praise Him day and night.

* Happy Voices, No. 22.

## LITTLE CHILDREN.

1 Sam. iii.   Matt. xix. 14; xxi. 16.

L. M.    **264.**    T. 22.

Though but a little child I am,
Yet I may praise the slaughter'd Lamb:
He loveth children tenderly,
He also loveth sinful me.

2. Yes, gracious Saviour, I believe
Thou wilt a little child receive;
For Thou didst bless them formerly,
And say, "Let children come to me."

3. Lord Jesus, unto me impart
A humble, meek, and docile heart;
O cleanse me in Thy precious blood,
Shed in my heart Thy love abroad.

4. Save me from liking what is ill,
Teach me to do Thy holy will;
Each day prepare me thro' Thy grace,
To meet Thee, and behold Thy face.

J. Cennick.

C. M.    **265.**    T. 14.

I am a little child, you see,
   My strength is little too,
But yet I fain would saved be;
   Lord, teach me what to do.

2. Thou, gracious Saviour, for my good
   Wast pleas'd a child to be,
And Thou didst shed Thy precious blood
   Upon the cross for me.

3. Come then, and take this heart of mine,
   Come, take me as I am,
I know that I by right am Thine,
   Thou loving, gracious Lamb.

4. If early Thou wilt take me hence,
   O that no harm will be;
Since endless bliss will then commence,
   When I shall live with Thee.

5. If Thou wilt have me longer stay,
   In years and stature grow;
Help me to serve Thee night and day,
   While I am here below.

*Zinzendorf.*

L. M.  **266.**  T. 22.

I will a little pilgrim be,
Resolv'd alone to follow Thee,
Thou Lamb of God, who now art gone
Up to Thy everlasting throne.

2. I will my heart to Thee resign,
Thine only be, O be Thou mine:
The world I leave and foolish play
To happiness to find the way.

3. My lips shall be employ'd to bless
The Lord who is my righteousness;
My pleasure, only to pursue
His steps, and His blest will to do.

4. So long I'll pray below to live,
Till I my pardon seal'd receive;
I then, when Jesus calls, shall die,
Or rather live eternally.

*Cennick.*

11s.  **267.**  T. 39.

Lord Jesus, we bless Thee that Thou wast a child,
And hast us thereby unto God reconcil'd:
We thank Thee for suffering and dying in pain,
For Thy being buried and rising again.

2. We thank Thee, that Thou wilt the children permit
To offer their praises and songs at Thy feet;
That Thou, Lord, dost deign their petitions to hear,
And always to help them and save them art near.

3. Thou wilt be our Saviour, Redeemer, and Friend,
Grant we may abide in Thy love to the end:
O render us truly obedient to Thee,
That we Thy dear children forever may be.

Cennick.

## 268.

7s.  T. 11.

Gentle Jesus, meek and mild,
Look upon a little child;
Pity my simplicity,
Suffer me to come to Thee.

2. Fain I would to Thee be brought;
Gracious God, forbid it not;
In the kingdom of Thy grace
Give a little child a place.

## 269.

6s. & 5s.*

Jesus, tender Saviour,
  Hast Thou died for me?
Make me very thankful
  In my heart to Thee.

2. When the sad, sad story
  Of Thy grief I read,
Make me very sorry
  For my sins, indeed.

3. Now I know Thou lovest
  And dost plead for me,
Make me very thankful
  In my prayers to Thee.

\* Happy Voices, No. 143.

## LITTLE CHILDREN.

4. Soon I hope in glory
   At Thy side to stand:
   Make me fit to meet Thee
   In that happy land.

H. M. [Lischer.] **270.**

When little Samuel woke,
   And heard his Maker's voice,
At every word He spoke,
   How much did he rejoice!
Oh, blessed, happy child! to find
The God of heaven so near and kind.

2. If God would speak to me,
   And say He was my friend,
How happy should I be!
   Oh, how would I attend!
The smallest sin I then should fear,
If God Almighty were so near.

3. And does he never speak?
   Oh, yes; for in His word
He bids me come and seek
   The God whom Samuel heard;
In almost every page I see,
The God of Samuel calls to me.

4. And I, beneath His care,
   May safely rest my head;
I know that God is there,
   To guard my humble bed:
And every sin I well may fear,
Since God Almighty is so near.

5. Like Samuel let me say,
   Whene'er I read His word,
"Speak, Lord: I would obey
   The voice that Samuel heard;
And when I in Thy house appear,
Speak, for Thy servant waits to hear."

LITTLE CHILDREN.

6s. & 5s.*
## 271.

Little drops of water,
  Little grains of sand,
Make the mighty ocean
  And the beauteous land.

2. And the little moments,
  Humble though they be,
Make the mighty ages
  Of eternity.

3. So our little errors
  Lead the soul away
From the paths of virtue
  Oft in sin to stray.

4. Little deeds of kindness,
  Little words of love,
Make our earth an Eden,
  Like the heaven above.

5. Little seeds of mercy,
  Sown by youthful hands,
Grow to bless the nations
  Far in heathen lands.

8s. 7s. & 4s.
## 272.
T. 585.

Saviour, like a shepherd lead us:
  Much we need Thy tender care;
In Thy pleasant pastures feed us,
  For our use Thy folds prepare,
    Blessed Jesus!
Thou hast bought us, Thine we are.

2. We are Thine: do Thou befriend us,
  Be the guardian of our way;

* Happy Voices, No. 131.

## LITTLE CHILDREN.

Keep Thy flock, from sin defend us,
  Seek us when we go astray.
    Blessed Jesus!
Hear Thy children when they pray.

3. Thou hast promised to receive us,
  Poor and sinful though we be;
Thou hast mercy to relieve us,
  Grace to cleanse, and power to free.
    Blessed Jesus!
Let us early turn to Thee.

4. Early let us seek Thy favor,
  Early let us do Thy will;
Holy Lord, our only Saviour,
  With Thy grace our bosoms fill.
    Blessed Jesus!
Thou hast loved us, love us still.

## 273.

P. M.*

I think when I read that sweet story of old,
  When Jesus was here among men,
How He call'd little children as lambs to His fold,
  I should like to have been with them then.

2. I wish that His hands had been plac'd on my head,
  That His arm had been thrown around me,
And that I had seen His kind look when He said,
  "Let the little ones come unto me."

3. Yet still to His footstool in prayer I may go,
  And ask for a share in His love;
And if I thus earnestly seek Him below,
  I shall see Him and hear Him above.

4. In that beautiful place He is gone to prepare
  For all who are washed and forgiven;
Full many dear children are gathering there,
  "For of such is the kingdom of heaven."

* Happy Voices, No. 27.

LITTLE CHILDREN.

5. But thousands and thousands who wander and fall,
  Never heard of that heavenly home;
I wish they could know there is room for them all,
  And that Jesus has bid them to come.

6. And oh, how I long for that glorious time,
  The sweetest and brightest and best,
When the dear little children of every clime,
  Shall crowd to His arms and be blest!

Mrs. Luke.

L. M.    **274.**    T. 22.

We are but young; yet we may sing
The praises of our heavenly king:
He made the earth, the sea, the sky,
And all the starry worlds on high.

2. We are but young; yet we must die;
Perhaps our latter end is nigh:
Lord, may we early seek Thy grace,
And find in Christ a hiding-place.

3. We are but young; we need a guide;
Jesus, in Thee we would confide;
Oh lead us in the path of truth,
Protect and bless our helpless youth.

4. We are but young; yet God has shed
Unnumber'd blessings on our head;
Then let our youth and riper days
Be all devoted to His praise.

6s. & 7s.    **275.**    T. 16.

Jesus, tender Shepherd, hear me;
  Bless Thy feeble lamb to-night:
Through the darkness be Thou near me;
  Keep me safe till morning light.

MISSIONARY.

2. All this day Thy hand has led me
   And I thank Thee for Thy care;
Kindly Thou hast clothed me, fed me,—
   Listen to my evening prayer.

3. May my sins be all forgiven,
   Bless the friends I love so well;
Take me, when I die, to heaven,
   Happy there with Thee to dwell.

                                    Duncan.

---

### MISSIONARY.

Matt. xxviii. 19.   Romans x. 14, 15.

## 276.

7s. & 6s.*                              T. 151.

From Greenland's icy mountains,
   From India's coral strand,
Where Afric's sunny fountains
   Roll down their golden sand;
From many an ancient river,
   From many a palmy plain,
They call us to deliver
   Their land from error's chain.

2. Shall we, whose souls are lighted
     With wisdom from on high,
   Shall we to men benighted,
     The lamp of life deny?
   Salvation! O salvation!
     The joyful sound proclaim,
   Till earth's remotest nation
     Has learn'd Messiah's name.

* Happy Voices, No. 125.

MISSIONARY.

3. Waft, waft, ye winds, his story,
  And you, ye waters roll,
Till like a sea of glory,
  It spreads from pole to pole;
Till o'er our ransom'd nature
  The Lamb for sinners slain,
Redeemer, King, Creator,
  In bliss returns to reign.

Heber.

H. M. [Lischer.] **277.**

Blow ye the trumpet, blow,
  The gladly solemn sound;
Let all the nations know,
  To earth's remotest bound,
The year of jubilee is come;
Return, ye ransom'd sinners, home.

2. Jesus, our great High Priest,
  Hath full atonement made:
Ye weary spirits, rest;
  Ye mournful souls, be glad;
The year of jubilee is come;
Return, ye ransom'd sinners, home.

3. Extol the Lamb of God—
  The all-atoning Lamb;
Redemption in His blood
  Throughout the world proclaim:
The year of jubilee is come;
Return, ye ransom'd sinners, home.

4. Ye who have sold for naught
  Your heritage above,
Shall have it back unbought,
  The gift of Jesus' love:
The year of jubilee is come;
Return, ye ransom'd sinners, home.

5. The gospel trumpet hear—
   The news of heavenly grace;
And, saved from earth, appear
   Before your Saviour's face:
The year of jubilee is come;
Return, ye ransom'd sinners, home.
                                C. Wesley.

## 278.   T. 11.

Hasten, Lord, the glorious time
   When, beneath Messiah's sway,
Every nation, every clime,
   Shall the gospel call obey!
Mightiest kings His power shall own,
   Heathen tribes His name adore;
Satan and his host o'erthrown,
   Bound in chains, shall hurt no more.

2. Then shall wars and tumults cease;
   Then be banished grief and pain;
Righteousness and joy and peace
   Undisturb'd shall ever reign!
Bless we, then, our gracious Lord,
   Ever praise His glorious name,
All His mighty acts record,
   All His wondrous love proclaim.

## 279.   T. 11.

Watchman, tell us of the night,
   What its signs of promise are.
Trav'ler, o'er yon mountain's height
   See the glory-beaming star.

2. Watchman, does its beauteous ray
   Aught of hope or joy foretell?
Trav'ler, yes, it brings the day—
   Promised day of Israel.

\* Happy Voices, No. 54.

MISSIONARY.

3. Watchman, tell us of the night;
   Higher yet that star ascends.
Trav'ler, blessedness and light,
   Peace and truth its course portends.

4. Watchman, will its beams alone
   Gild the spot that gave them birth?
Trav'ler, ages are its own;
   See, it bursts o'er all the earth.

5. Watchman, tell us of the night,
   For the morning seems to dawn.
Trav'ler, darkness takes its flight;
   Doubt and terror are withdrawn.

6. Watchman, let thy wand'rings cease;
   Hie thee to thy quiet home.
Trav'ler, lo! the Prince of Peace,
   Lo! the Son of God is come.

Bowring.

7s. & 6s.    **280.**    T. 151.

When shall the voice of singing
   Flow joyfully along?
When hill and valley ringing
   With one triumphant song,
Proclaim the contest ended,
   And Him who once was slain,
Again to earth descended,
   In righteousness to reign?

2. Then from the craggy mountains
     The sacred shout shall fly;
   And shady vales and fountains
     Shall echo the reply.
   High tower and lowly dwelling
     Shall send the chorus round,
   All hallelujah swelling
     In one eternal sound!

Pratt's Collection.

## 281.

7s. & 6s.   T. 151.

Now be the Gospel banner,
  In every land, unfurled;
And be the shout, "Hosanna!"
  Re-echoed through the world;
Till every isle and nation,
  Till every tribe and tongue,
Receives the great salvation,
  And joins the happy throng.

2. Yes, Thou shalt reign forever,
  O Jesus, King of kings!
Thy light, Thy love, Thy favor,
  Each ransomed captive sings:
The isles for Thee are waiting,
  The deserts learn Thy praise,
The hills and valleys greeting,
  The song responsive raise.

Hastings.

## 282.

L. M.   T. 22.

Sovereign of worlds! display Thy power,
Be this Thy Zion's favor'd hour,
Bid the bright morning star arise,
And point the heathen to the skies.

2. Set up Thy throne where Satan reigns,
On Afric's shore, on India's plains,
On wilds, and continents unknown,
And make the universe Thine own.

3. Speak! and the world shall hear Thy voice;
Speak! and the desert shall rejoice;
Scatter the gloom of heathen night,
And bid all nations hail the light.

## MISSIONARY.

11s.     **283.**     T. 39.

Oh, send forth the Bible, more precious than gold!
Let no one presume this best gift to withhold;
It speaks to all nations in language so plain,
That he who will read it true wisdom may gain.

2. It points us to heaven, where the righteous will go;
It warns us to shun the dark regions of woe;
It shows us the evil and dangers of sin,
And opens a fountain for cleansing within.

3. It tells us of One who is mighty to save,
Who died on the cross, and arose from the grave,
Who dwelleth on high in that holy abode,
Interceding for man with a pardoning God.

4. It tells us that all will awake from the tomb,
Bids sinners reflect on a judgment to come;
It tells us that mansions of bliss are prepared,
The hope of believers,—their glorious award.

5. Oh, who would neglect such a volume as this,
That warns us from danger, invites us to bliss?
Send forth the blest Bible earth's region's around,
Wherever the footsteps of man shall be found.

P. M.*     **284.**

Hear the royal proclamation,
The glad tidings of salvation,
Publishing to every creature,
To the ruin'd sons of nature—

CHORUS.
Jesus reigns, He reigns victorious,
Over heaven and earth most glorious,
Jesus reigns!

\* Golden Chain, p. 40.

2. See the royal banner flying,
Hear the heralds loudly crying:
"Rebel sinners, royal favor
Now is offered by the Saviour.
   CHORUS.

3. "Turn unto the Lord most holy;
Shun the paths of vice and folly;
Turn, or you are lost forever;
Oh, now turn to God the Saviour.
   CHORUS.

4. "Here is wine and milk and honey;
Come and purchase without money;
Mercy flowing like a fountain,
Streaming from the holy mountain!"
   CHORUS.

5. Shout, ye tongues of every nation,
To the bounds of the creation—
Shout the praise of Judah's Lion,
The Almighty Prince of Zion.
   CHORUS.

## 285.

10s.*

Over the ocean-wave, far, far away,
There the poor heathen live, waiting for day;
Groping in ignorance, dark as the night,
No blessed Bible to give them the light.
   CHORUS.
 Pity them, pity them, Christians at home,
 Haste with the bread of life, hasten and come!

2. Bowing to idol gods, daily they pray:
"Pity us, Juggernaut! we've given away
Lives of our children dear, thee to appease,
Give to us, give to us tokens of peace."
   CHORUS.

\* Golden Chain, p. 41.

3. Here, in this happy land, we have the light
Shining from God's own word, free, pure, and bright;
Shall we not send to them Bibles to read,
Teachers, and preachers, and all that they need?
CHORUS.

4. Then when the mission-ships glad tidings bring,
List! as that heathen band joyfully sing:
"Over the ocean wave, oh! see them come,
Bringing the bread of life, guiding us home."
CHORUS.

8s. 7s. & 4s.  **286.**  T. 585.

O'er the realms of pagan darkness
  Let the eye of pity gaze;
See the thronging, wandering nations,
  Lost in sin's bewildering maze:
    Darkness brooding
On the face of all the earth.

2. Light of them that sit in darkness,
  Rise and shine! Thy blessings bring:
Light to lighten all the Gentiles!
  Rise with healing in Thy wing:
    To Thy brightness
Let all kings and nations come.

3. May the heathen, now adoring
  Idol-gods of wood and stone,
Come, and worshiping before Him,
  Serve the living God alone:
    Let Thy glory
Fill the earth as floods the sea.

4. Thou, to whom all power is given,
  Speak the word: at Thy command,
Let the heralds of Thy mercy
  Spread Thy name from land to land:
    Lord, be with them
Always, to the end of time.
          Cotterell.

## ANNIVERSARY.

7s. & 6s.
### 287.
T. 151.

To Thee, O blessed Saviour,
  Our grateful songs we raise;
Oh, tune our hearts and voices,
  Thy holy name to praise:
'Tis by Thy sov'reign mercy
  We're here allowed to meet;
To join with friends and teachers,
  Thy blessing to entreat.

2. Lord, guide and bless our teachers,
  Who labor for our good;
And may the Holy Scriptures
  By us be understood;
Oh, may our hearts be given
  To Thee, our glorious King;
That we may meet in heaven,
  Thy praises there to sing.

3. And may the precious gospel
  Be published all abroad,
Till the benighted heathen
  Shall know and serve the Lord;
Till o'er the wide creation,
  The rays of truth shall shine,
And nations, now in darkness,
  Arise to light divine.

8s. & 7s.
### 288.
T. 167.

Precious Saviour, of salvation
  We, this festal day would sing,
And would make our celebration
  With our Saviour's praises ring.

## ANNIVERSARY.

'Tis Thy mercy that hath led us
  To the Sabbath school we love;
And our teachers there have fed us
  With the manna from above.

2. Precious Saviour, 'tis Thy blessing
  Cheers us in the morn of life;
Helps us onward to be pressing,
  'Mid earth's sorrows and its strife;
Guards from fascinating pleasures,
  That would lead our feet astray;
Sets before us heavenly treasures,
  While we walk the narrow way.

3. Precious Saviour, we adore Thee,
  For Thy many mercies shown:
Let our praises come before Thee,—
  Find acceptance at Thy throne.
Thus our songs, to heaven ascending,
  Join with those of saints above,
And with angel-voices blending,
  Celebrate redeeming love.

P. M.*  **289.**

Preserved by Thine almighty power,
  O Lord, our Maker, Saviour, King!
And brought to see this happy hour,
  We come Thy praises here to sing.
  Happy day, happy day,
  Here in Thy courts we'll gladly stay,
  And at Thy footstool humbly pray,
  That Thou wouldst take our sins away.
  Happy day, happy day,
  When Christ shall wash our sins away.

2. We praise Thee for Thy constant care,
  For life preserved, for mercies given;

* Happy Voices, No. 43.

ANNIVERSARY.

Oh, may we still those mercies share,
  And taste the joys of sins forgiven!
    Happy day, &c.

3. And when on earth our days are done,
  Grant, Lord, that we at length may join,
  Teachers and scholars round Thy throne,
    The song of Moses and the Lamb.
      Happy day, &c.

## 290.

11s.*     T. 39.

The Sunday school army has gather'd once more;
Its numbers are greater than ever before;
Its banners are spread, and shall never be furl'd,
Till the Prince of salvation has conquer'd the world.

CHORUS.

(Sing! sing! for the army is on its bright way
To the homes of the blest and the mansions of day.)

2. We fight against evil and battle with wrong,
Our sword is the Bible, both trusty and strong;
Our watchword is prayer, and faith is our shield,
And never, no, never to our foes will we yield.

3. In the midst of our conflicts we'll think of the Lord,
Who died on the cross, and from death was restored,
To save us from sin, and to give us a place
With the angels who always behold His bright face.

4. To Jesus, our Captain, hosannas we raise,
And join with our teachers in singing His praise;
His soldiers we are, and His soldiers will be,
Till we lay down our armor, and death sets us free.
                           E. S. Porter.

* S. S. Hosanna, p. 68.

ANNIVERSARY.

8s. & 7s.*
## 291.
T. 16.

Days and weeks and months returning,
  Bear us gently down life's way:
Still their lesson we are learning
  With each anniversary day.
  CHORUS.
  We hail this day, so full of joy,
    And greet it with a song.

2. Glad our hearts and glad our voices,
    Joy controls the hasting hour;
None so sad but he rejoices
    'Neath to-day's controlling power.

3. Glad for classmates and for teachers,
    Guiding us with gentle rule,
Glad for all the gifts that reach us
    Through our own loved Sunday-school.

4. Yet, though glad, we'll still remember
    What the moments always say:
Life must have its cold December,
    Just as surely as its May.

5. Let us not forget the meaning
    Days like these forever wear:
One more field has had its gleaning,
    One more sheaf our arms should bear.

7s. & 6s.
## 292.
T. 151.

We bring no glittering treasures,
  No gems from earth's deep mine;
We come, with simple measures,
  To chant Thy love divine.
Children, Thy favors sharing,
  Their voice of thanks would raise;
Father, accept our offering,
  Our song of grateful praise.

* S. S. Hosanna, p. 148. P. S. S. Coll., p. 201.

2. The dearest gift of heaven,
   Love's written word of Truth,
To us is early given,
   To guide our steps in youth:
We hear the wondrous story,
   The tale of Calvary;
We read of homes in glory,
   From sin and sorrow free.

3. Redeemer, grant Thy blessing:
   Oh, teach us how to pray,
That each, Thy fear possessing,
   May tread life's onward way;
Then where the pure are dwelling
   We hope to meet again,
And, sweeter numbers swelling,
   For ever praise Thy name.

## PATRIOTIC HYMNS.

**293.**

6s. & 4s. [America.]

My country, 'tis of thee,
Sweet land of liberty,
   Of thee I sing;
Land where my fathers died,
Land of the pilgrim's pride,
From every mountain-side
   Let freedom ring.

2. My native country, thee,
Land of the noble free,
   Thy name I love;
I love thy rocks and rills,
Thy woods and templed hills,
My heart with rapture thrills,
   Like that above.

3. Let music swell the breeze,
And ring from all the trees
   Sweet freedom's song:
Let mortal tongues awake,
Let all that breathe partake,
Let rocks their silence break,
   The sound prolong.

4. Our fathers' God, to Thee,
Author of liberty,
   To Thee we sing;
Long may our land be bright
With freedom's holy light;
Protect us by Thy might,
   Great God, our King.

S. F. Smith.

## 294.

6s. 7s. & 4s.     T. 585.

God of every land and nation,
   On this glorious Jubilee,
Let the incense of oblation,
   From each heart arise to Thee.
     Save our country:
   Long preserve her liberty.

2. Let Thy richest blessings ever
   Rest upon our happy land;
May no fierce contention sever
   The confederated band:
     In sweet union
May we still unshaken stand.

3. May we all be safely guided,
   Saviour, by Thy gracious will:
When life's storms shall have subsided,
   And our tongues in death are still,
     May we praise Thee,
Where immortal glories thrill.

## ON OPENING A NEW SCHOOL ROOM.

### 295.

L. M.     T. 22.

Great God of nations, now to Thee,
Our hymn of gratitude we raise;
That Thou hast made this nation free,
We offer Thee our song of praise.

2. Thy name we bless, Almighty God,
For all the kindness Thou hast shown
To this fair land, by pilgrims trod,—
This land we fondly call our own.

3. Here freedom spreads its banner wide,
And casts its soft and hallowed ray:
Here Thou our fathers' steps didst guide,
In safety through their dangerous way.

4. We praise Thee, that the gospel's light
Through all our land its radiance sheds,—
Dispels the shades of error's night,
And heavenly blessings round us spreads.

---

## ON OPENING A NEW SCHOOL ROOM.

### 296.

L. M.     T. 22.

Great God! Thy watchful care we bless,
Which gives our feeble plans success;
Here may we oft delight to meet
Our youthful charge at Jesus' feet.

2. These walls we to Thine honor raise;
Long may they echo with Thy praise!
Do Thou, descending, fill the place
With choicest tokens of Thy grace.

3. Here may the great Redeemer reign,
With all the graces of His train;
While power divine His word imparts,
To conquer youthful sinners' hearts.

THE YEAR.

4. And, in the great, decisive day,
When God the nations shall survey,
May it before the world appear,
That crowds were born for glory here.

7s.

## 297.

T. 11.

Glory to the Father give,
God in whom we move and live;
Children's prayers He deigns to hear,
Children's songs delight his ear.

2. Glory to the Son we bring,
Christ our Prophet, Priest, and King;
Children raise your sweetest strain
To the Lamb, for he was slain.

3. Glory to the Holy Ghost;
Be this day a Pentecost:
Children's minds may He inspire,
Touch their tongues with holy fire.

4. Glory in the highest be
To the blessed Trinity,
For the Gospel from above,
For the word, that "God is love."

*Montgomery.*

## NEW YEAR.

Psalm xc.

7s. Double.

## 298.

T. 11 or 205.

While with ceaseless course the sun
  Hasted through the former year,
Many souls their race have run,
  Never more to meet us here.

## THE YEAR.

Fix'd in their eternal state,
  They have done with all below;
We a little longer wait,
  But how little none can know.

2. As the winged arrow flies
  Speedily the mark to find,
As the lightning from the skies
  Darts, and leaves no trace behind,
Swiftly thus our fleeting days
  Bear us down life's rapid stream;
Upward, Lord, our spirits raise:
  All below is but a dream.

3. Thanks for mercies past receive;
  Pardon of our sins renew;
Teach us henceforth how to live
  With eternity in view,
Bless Thy word to young and old;
  Fill us with a Saviour's love;
And, when life's short tale is told,
  May we dwell with Thee above.

C. M.

## 299.

T 14.

Again another fleeting year
  Of my short life is past;
I cannot long continue here,
  And this may be my last.

2. Much of my dubious life is gone,
  Nor will return again;
And swift my passing moments run,
  The few that yet remain.

3. Now a new scene of time begins;
  Press on, my soul, to heaven;
Seek pardon of thy former sins,
  By Christ it will be giv'n.

MORNING.

Devoutly yield thyself to God,
And on His grace depend;
Unwearied walk the heavenly road,
Nor doubt a happy end.

*La Trobe.*

L. M.     **300.**     T. 22.

Great God! we sing that mighty hand,
By which supported still we stand;
The opening year Thy mercy shows;
Let mercy crown it till it close.

2. By day, by night, at home, abroad,
Still we are guarded by our God;
By His incessant bounty fed,
By His unerring counsel led.

3. In scenes exalted or depressed,
Be Thou our joy, and Thou our rest;
Thy goodness all our hope shall raise,
Adored through all our changing days.

4. When death shall interrupt our songs,
And seal in silence mortal tongues,
Oh, may Thy praise our lips employ
In the eternal world of joy.

*Doddridge.*

---

**MORNING.**

Psalm v. 3.

L. M.     **301.**     T. 22.

Awake, my soul, and with the sun
Thy daily stage of duty run;
Shake off dull sloth, and early rise
To pay thy morning sacrifice.

2. Thy former misspent time redeem,
Each present day thy last esteem;
Thy talents to improve take care,
For the great day thyself prepare.

3. In conversation be sincere,
Keep conscience as the noon-day clear;
For God's all-seeing eye surveys
Thy secret thoughts, thy works and ways.

4. Glory to God, who safe hath kept,
And hath refreshed me while I slept:
Grant, Lord, when I from death shall wake,
I may of heavenly bliss partake.

5. Lord, I my vows to thee renew,
Disperse my sins as morning dew,
Guard my first springs of thought and will,
And with Thyself my spirit fill.

6. Direct, control, suggest this day
All I design, or do, or say;
That all my powers, with all their might,
In Thy sole glory may unite.

Kenn.

C. M. **302.** T. 14.

What secret hand, at morning light,
  By stealth unseals mine eye,
Draws back the curtain of the night,
  And opens earth and sky?

2. 'Tis Thine, my God,—the same that kept
  My resting hours from harm;
No ill came nigh me, for I slept
  Beneath the Almighty's arm.

3. 'Tis thine,—my daily bread that brings,
  Like manna scatter'd round,
And clothes me, as the lily springs
  In beauty from the ground.

4. This is the hand that shap'd my frame,
   And gave my pulse to beat;
That bare me oft through flood and flame,
   Through tempest, cold, and heat.

5. In death's dark valley though I stray,
   'Twould there my steps attend,
Guide with the staff my lonely way,
   And with the rod defend.

6. May that dear hand uphold me still,
   Thro' life's uncertain race,
To bring me to Thine holy hill,
   And to Thy dwelling-place.

J. Montgomery.

# 303. T. 10.

My soul, awake, and render
To God, thy great defender,
Thy prayer and adoration
For His kind preservation.

2. With joy I still discover
Thy light, O Lord, my Saviour;
My thanks shall be the spices
Of morning sacrifices.

3. Bless me, this day, Lord Jesus,
And be to me propitious;
Grant me Thy kind protection
From every sin's infection.

4. Bless every thought and action;
Afford me Thy direction;
To Thee alone be tending
Beginning, middle, ending.

5. Be Thou my only treasure,
Fulfil in me Thy pleasure;
May I in every station
Give Thee due adoration.

Gerhard.

MORNING.

## 304.
T. 79.

May Jesus' grace and blessing
Attend me without ceasing:
Thus I stretch out my hand,
And do that work with pleasure,
Which, in my call and measure,
My God for me to do ordain'd.

*Mathesius.*

## 305.
T. 22.

O timely happy, timely wise
Hearts that with rising morn arise!
Eyes that the beam celestial view,
Which evermore makes all things new.

2. New every morning is the love
Our wakening and uprising prove,
Through sleep and darkness safely brought,
Restored to life, and power, and thought.

3. New mercies, each returning day,
Hover around us while we pray;
New perils past, new sins forgiven,
New thoughts of God, new hopes of heaven.

4. If on our daily course our mind
Be set to hallow all we find,
New treasures still, of countless price,
God will provide for sacrifice.

5. The trivial round, the common task,
Will furnish all we ought to ask;—
Room to deny ourselves; a road
To bring us daily nearer God.

6. Only, O Lord, in Thy dear love
Fit us for perfect rest above;
And help us, this and every day,
To live more nearly as we pray.

*Keble.*

MORNING.

7s.     **306.**     T. 11.

Now the shades of night are gone;
Now the morning light is come:
Lord, may we be Thine to-day,
Drive the shades of sin away.

2. Fill our souls with heavenly light,
Banish doubt, and clear our sight;
In Thy service, Lord, to-day
May we stand, and watch, and pray.

3. Keep our haughty passions bound,
Save us from our foes around,
Going out and coming in,
Keep us safe from every sin.

L. M.     **307.**     T. 22.

Be with me, Lord, where'er I go,
Teach me what Thou would'st have me do;
Suggest whate'er I think this day,
Direct me in the narrow way.

2. Prevent me lest I harbor pride,
Lest I in my own strength confide;
Show me my weakness, let me see
I have my power, my all, from Thee.

3. Enrich me always with Thy love,
My kind protector ever prove:
Lord, put Thy seal upon my breast,
And let Thy Spirit on me rest.

4. Assist and teach me how to pray,
Incline my nature to obey;
What Thou abhorrest, let me flee,
And only love what pleaseth Thee.

Cennick.

## EVENING.

Psalm cxli. 2.

8s. & 7s.    **308.**    T. 16.

Saviour, breathe an evening-blessing
Ere repose our spirits seal;
Sin and want we come confessing,
Thou canst save, and Thou canst heal.

2. Though destruction walk around us,
Though the arrows past us fly,
Angel-guards from Thee surround us;
We are safe, if Thou art nigh.

3. Though the night be dark and dreary,
Darkness cannot hide from Thee;
Thou, our Shepherd, never weary,
Watchest where Thy people be.

*Edmeston.*

L. M.    **309.**    T. 22.

Sun of my soul, Thou Saviour dear,
It is not night if Thou be near;
Oh! may no earth-born cloud arise
To hide Thee from Thy servant's eyes!

2. When the soft dews of kindly sleep
My wearied eyelids gently steep,
Be my last thought, how sweet to rest
For ever on my Saviour's breast!

3. If some poor wandering child of Thine
Have spurned to-day the voice divine;
Now, Lord, the gracious work begin,
Let him no more lie down in sin!

4. Watch by the sick, enrich the poor
With blessings from Thy boundless store;
Be every mourner's sleep to-night,
Like infant's slumbers, pure and light!

EVENING.

5. Come near and bless us when we wake,
Ere through the world our way we take;
Till in the ocean of Thy love
We lose ourselves in Heaven above.

*Keble.*

L. M. **310.** T. 22.

All praise to Thee, my God, this night,
For all the blessings of the light;
Keep me, O keep me, King of kings,
Beneath Thy own almighty wings.

2. Forgive me, Lord, for Thy dear Son,
The ill that I this day have done,
That with the world, myself, and Thee,
I, ere I sleep, at peace may be.

3. Teach me to live, that I may dread
The grave as little as my bed;
Teach me to die, that so I may
Rise glorious at the judgment-day.

4. O may my soul on Thee repose,
And may sweet sleep my eye-lids close,
Sleep, that may me more vigorous make
To serve my God when I awake.

5. When in the night I sleepless lie,
My soul with heavenly thoughts supply;
Let no ill dreams disturb my rest,
No powers of darkness me molest.

*Kenn.*

L. M. **311.** T. 22.

The hours' decline and setting sun
Show that my course this day is run;
The evening-shade and silent night
My weary limbs to rest invite.

2. I now my soul and frail abode
Humbly commit to Israel's God,
To Him who slumbers not nor sleeps,
And who His own in safety keeps.

3. Where'er I Thee this day did grieve,
O Lord, me graciously forgive;
And with a mind from trouble freed,
Let me sleep in Thy peace indeed.

C. M.

## 312.

T. 14.

The hour of sleep is now at hand,
  My spirit calls for rest;
O that my pillow may be found
  The dear Redeemer's breast.

2. This night my longing soul with Christ
  Would take up her abode,
I gladly would myself divest
  Of everything but God.

3. The nightly watches would I spend
  In fellowship above;
Would hold communion with my Lord,
  And feast upon His love.

4. Dead to the world when I'm asleep,
  I'd be alive to God;
My soul would rest at peace with Him
  Who bought me with His blood.

5. O may I then of Christ this night
  Be happily possess'd,
With holy angels round my bed,
  And Jesus for my guest.

## 313.

Now I lay me down to sleep
  I pray the Lord my soul to keep;
If I should die before I wake,
  I pray the Lord my soul to take. Amen.

## 314.    T. 68.

  Jesus, hear our prayer,
    For Thy children care;
While we sleep, protect and bless us,
With Thy pardon now refresh us;
    Leave Thy peace divine
    With us, we are Thine.

Zinzendorf.

---

## BEFORE AND AFTER MEALS.

Psalm cxlvi. 7.    Matt. vi. 11.

C. M.      **315.**      T. 14.

Thee we address in humble prayer,
  Vouchsafe Thy gifts to crown,
Father of all, Thy children hear,
  And send a blessing down.

2. May we enjoy Thy saving grace,
  Thy goodness taste and see,
Athirst for blood-bought righteousness,
  And hungry after Thee.

C. Wesley.

7s.      **316.**      T. 11.

Jesus' mercies never fail,
This we prove at every meal:
Lord, we thank Thee for Thy grace,
Gladly join to sing Thy praise.

2. Lord, the gifts Thou dost bestow,
Can refresh and cheer us too;
But no gift can to the heart
Be what Thou our Saviour art.

3. Praise our God! it is but just;
He hath rais'd us from the dust,
Gave us being, gave us breath,
Saves us from eternal death.

J. Angelus.

## 317. T. 79.

What praise to Thee, my Saviour,
Is due for every favor,
 Ev'n for my daily food:
Each crumb Thou dost allow me,
With gratitude shall bow me,
 Accounting all for me too good.

L. M.

## 318. T. 22.

Be present at our table, Lord;
Be here and every where ador'd:
From Thy all-bounteous hand our food
May we receive with gratitude.

2. We humbly thank Thee, Lord our God,
For all Thy gifts on us bestow'd;
And pray Thee, graciously to grant
The food which day by day we want.

---

Come, Lord Jesus, our guest to be,
And bless the gifts bestowed by Thee.

---

Be present, Lord, at this repast,
And bless what Thou provided hast.

## TEMPERANCE.

1 Cor. ix. 25.  1 Peter i. 6.

6s. & 4s. [America.] **319.**

Now let our hearts rejoice,
And every youthful voice
   Its tribute raise;
That, from this happy throng
May swell a thankful song,
To Him to whom belong
   Honor and praise.

2. The Lord, in bounty, gives
To every thing that lives,
   Throughout the land,
Waters, whose taste is sweet,—
Fountains, the eye to greet,—
The crystal streams we meet
   On every hand.

3. He gives the dew and rain,
Falling on hill and plain,
   And every where,—
Spreading a robe of green,
In beauty, o'er each scene;
Filling, with joy serene,
   The balmy air.

4. Then let our hearts rejoice,
While, with united voice,
   We raise our song;
And may He in the ways
Of virtue and of grace
Keep us, through all our days,
   Steadfast and strong.

TEACHERS' MEETINGS.

S. M.   **320.**   T 595 or 582.

Mourn for the thousands slain,
  The youthful and the strong;
Mourn for the wine-cup's fatal reign,
  And the deluded throng.

2. Mourn for the tarnished gem—
  For reason's light divine,
Quenched from the soul's bright diadem,
  Where God hath bid it shine.

3. Mourn for the ruined soul—
  Eternal life and light
Lost by the fiery, maddening bowl,
  And turned to hopeless night.

4. Mourn for the lost,—but call,
  Call to the strong, the free;
Rouse them to shun that dreadful fall,
  And to the refuge flee.

5. Mourn for the lost,—but pray,
  Pray to our God above,
To break the fell destroyer's sway,
  And show His saving love.

---

### TEACHERS' MEETINGS.

Daniel xii. 3. Matthew xviii 20. Romans xii. 7.

L. M.   **321.**   T. 22.

Be present with Thy servants, Lord,
We look to Thee with one accord;
Refresh and strengthen us anew,
And bless what in Thy name we do.

2. O teach us all Thy perfect will
To understand and to fulfil:
When human insight fails, give light;
This will direct our steps aright.

3. The Lord's joy be our strength and stay,
In our employ from day to day;
Our thoughts and our activity
Thro' Jesus' merits hallow'd be.

L. M.  **322.**  T. 32.

In mercy, Lord, this grace bestow,
That in Thy service we may do,
With gladness and a willing mind,
Whatever is for us assign'd.

2. Grant we, impelled by Thy love,
In smallest things may faithful prove;
Till we depart, we wish to be
Devoted wholly unto Thee.

*Zinzendorf.*

8s & 7s.  **323.**  T. 16.

Saviour—King! in hallowed union,
  At Thy sacred feet we bow:
Heart with heart, in blest communion,
  Join to crave Thy favor now.

2. Heavenly Fount! thy streams of blessing
  Oft have cheered us on our way:
By thy power and grace unceasing,
  We continue to this day.

3. Raise we, then, in glad emotion,
  Thankful lays; and while we sing,
Vow a pure, a full devotion
  To Thy work, O Saviour-King.

## TEACHERS' MEETINGS.

4. When we tell the wondrous story
 Of Thy rich, exhaustless love,
Send Thy Spirit, Lord of glory,
 On the youthful heart to move.

5. Oh that He, the Ever-living,
 May descend, as fruitful rain;
Till the wilderness, reviving,
 Blossoms as the rose again.

6. Then may they whom we have guided,
 Life's tempestuous ocean o'er,
In the home Thou hast provided,
 Meet us, to depart no more.

7. There, beside the crystal river,
 Flowing from th' eternal throne,
Shall arise to Thee for ever,
 Praise more sweet than earth has known.

L. M.
### 324.
T. 21.

Fountain of wisdom, source of truth,
Oh, listen, while we bend the knee;
And grant that we, before we teach,
May first be truly taught of Thee.

2. Grant us a constant prayerful mind;
And if, perchance, no fruits appear,
Still may we labor on in faith,
From month to month, from year to year.

3. Still may we love those priceless souls,
And imitate the incarnate Son,
Who meeting scorn and cold neglect
And faithlessness, did yet love on.

4. And grant, O God, that while we feed,
Our hungering spirits may be fed;
And while another's steps we lead,
Our own may into truth be led;—

5. That, laboring in this harvest-field,
Our souls may be in blessing blest;
Until the Lord shall come, and take
Teachers and taught to endless rest.

L. M.      **325.**      T. 22.

Here, gracious God, low at Thy feet,
Friends to the young and Thee, we meet;
Joined by the cord of mutual love,
Bound to our common Friend above.

2. Our hearts Thy throne of grace address:
Smile on our school, the children bless;
For Jesus' sake, who once on earth
Appeared, a child of lowly birth.

3. Bless all the plans which we devise;
May they be useful, good and wise;
Whilst we our humble labors bend
Thy glorious kingdom to extend.

4. May wisdom, zeal, and love inspire
Our bosoms with their purest fire;
While faith on Thine own word relies,
And hope looks joyful to the skies.

5. Grant us Thy presence, God of grace,
Now, while we meet before Thy face;
That we may feel, ere we depart,
Thy love diffused through every heart.

L. M.      **326.**      T. 22.

Great God, our feeble efforts own,
And crown our labors with success;
Grant that the seed, in weakness sown,
May soon be raised in righteousness.

2. To those we teach Thy mercy show,
And let their souls before Thee live;
For we may plant, and water too,
But Thou alone canst increase give.

3. Seal our instructions on each heart,
And teach them to observe Thy ways;
Lead them to choose the better part,
And serve Thee in their youthful days.

4. Then we and they, when time shall end,
Shall joyful meet Thee in the sky;
Before Thy throne of glory bend,
And praise Thee through eternity.

S. M.

## 327.

T. 582 or 595.

Sow in the morn thy seed
  At eve hold not thy hand,
To doubt and fear give thou no heed,
  Broadcast it round the land.

2. Beside all waters sow,
  The high-way furrows stock,
Drop it where thorns and thistles grow,
  Scatter it on the rock.

3. The good, the fruitful ground,
  Expect not here nor there;
O'er hill and dale, by spots 'tis found:
  Go forth, then, everywhere.

4. Thou know'st not which may thrive,
  The late or early sown;
Grace keeps the precious germ alive,
  When and wherever strown.

5. And duly shall appear,
  In verdure, beauty, strength,
The tender blade, the stalk, the ear,
  And the full corn at length.

6. Thou cans't not toil in vain:
    Cold, heat, and moist, and dry,
Shall foster and mature the grain,
    For garners in the sky.

7. Then, when the glorious end—
    The day of God—is come,
The angel-reapers shall descend,
    To take the harvest home.

Montgomery.

C. M.  **328.**  T. 14.

Teacher divine, we bow the knee,
    Dependent, at Thy throne,
Our fervent cry we raise to Thee:
    Ah, leave us not alone.

2. In vain we teach unless Thy grace
    Instruct each tender heart:
Then deign to hear, hide not Thy face,
    Thy Spirit, Lord, impart.

3. Without Thee we can nothing do,
    Our weakness we confess;
Be Thou our strength and wisdom too,
    And thus our labors bless.

4. And may the sacred tie of love
    Bind us together here,—
A foretaste give of joys above,
    Life's pilgrimage to cheer.

5. Thus, while on earth, we would adore;
    When death shall close our eyes,
May teachers, scholars, meet once more,
    Transplanted to the skies.

## TEACHERS' MEETINGS.

S. M.

### 329.

T. 505.

How serious is the charge
  To train the youthful mind!
'Tis God alone can give a heart
  To such a work inclined.

2. May we, in Christian bonds,
  The Christian's name adorn
By active deeds for public good;
  Nor heed the sinner's scorn.

3. While wicked men unite
  Our youth to lead aside,
'Tis ours to show them wisdom's path,—
  In wisdom's path to guide.

4. Dependent, Lord, on Thee,
  Our humble means to bless,
We gladly join our hearts and hands,
  And look for large success.

L. M.

### 330.

T. 22.

Except the Lord our labors bless
In vain shall we desire success;
Except His guardian power restrain,
The watchman waketh but in vain.

2. 'Tis useless toil our stores to keep,
Early to rise, and late to sleep,
Unless the Lord, who reigns on high,
His providential care supply.

3. Grant, Lord, that we may ever flee
For guidance and for help to Thee;
Thy blessing ask, whate'er we do,
And in Thy strength our work pursue.

L. M.

## 331.

T. 22.

Where two or three, with sweet accord,
Obedient to their sovereign Lord,
Meet to recount His acts of grace,
And offer solemn prayer and praise:

2. "There," saith the Saviour, "I will be,
Amidst this little company;
To them I will unveil my face,
And shed my glories round the place."

3. We meet at Thy command, O Lord,
Relying on Thy faithful word;
Now send Thy Spirit from above,
And fill our hearts with heavenly love.

8s. 7s. & 4s.

## 332.

T. 588.

Blessed Saviour! Thou hast told us,
 In the midst of two or three,
Thou art present to behold us,
 If we humbly call on Thee;
Blessed promise,—blessed promise,—
 May we Thy salvation see!

2. O instruct us, gracious Master,
 While Thy tender lambs we guide;
May we lead them to green pasture,
 By the living water's side,
Where the fountain of salvation
 Pours its soul-refreshing tide.

3. Lord, we bring our charge before Thee,
 Little ones of Thine own fold;
Teach them, Saviour, to adore Thee,
 As those children did of old,
Who sang praises, high hosannas,
 When the hearts of men were cold.

4. Haste the time when all the islands
   In the bosom of the sea,
And the lowlands, plains and highlands,
   Shall resound with praise to Thee;
And the children of all nations
   Shall their God and Saviour see.

---

OPENING AND CLOSING SCHOOL.

## 333.

S. M.  T. 595.

We come to sing Thy praise,
   We meet to offer prayer,
We come to learn of wisdom's ways;
   Blest Saviour! meet us here!

2. Thy Spirit, Lord, impart,
   That, while we raise the voice
In sacred melody, the heart
   In praises may rejoice.

3. And when the offer'd prayer
   Goes upward to Thy throne,
May we in each petition share,
   And make each want our own.

4. And as Thy Holy Word
   We study and are taught,
Let every truth and precept, Lord,
   Be with Thy blessing fraught.

5. So shall the hours we spend
   Together in this place,
Through all our future being send
   The savor of Thy grace.

## 334.

S. M.  T. 22.

Assembled in our school once more,
O Lord, Thy blessing we implore;
We meet to read, and sing, and pray,
Be with us then throughout Thy day.

2. Our fervent prayer to Thee ascends,
For parents, teachers, foes and friends,
And when we in Thy house appear,
Help us to worship in Thy fear.

3. When we on earth shall meet no more,
May we above to glory soar,
And praise Thee in more lofty strains,
Where one eternal Sabbath reigns.

## 335.

S. M.  T. 582 or 595.

Lord fix our wandering thoughts,
  Thy sacred word to hear
With deep attention and with love,
  With reverence and with fear.

2. Let us remember still
  That God is present here;
And let our hearts be all engaged
  When we draw near in prayer.

3. And when the humble notes
  Of praise our lips employ,
Give us to taste the sweet delight
  Which saints in heaven enjoy.

4. Oh, may Thy sacred word
  Sink deep in every breast,
And let us all by grace be brought
  To Christ, the promised rest.

OPENING AND CLOSING SCHOOL.

C. M.
### 336.
T. 14.

And now another hour is past,
 Of kind instruction given;
And this, perhaps, may be the last
 On this side hell or heaven!

2. And is it so? How dread the thought,
 And yet indeed how true!
If I could feel it as I ought,
 This day, what should I do?

3. O surely prize it more and more,
 And pray that God would give
A death of gain, if life be o'er,
 And blessing, if I live.

8s. 7s. & 4s.
### 337.
T. 585.

Now is past the time of teaching,
 Ended is the hour we love,
Hush'd the voice of friends, beseeching
 Us to seek for joys above:
  Precious Sabbaths!
Swiftly, oh, they swiftly move.

2. Wake, then, every tender feeling,
 Ere from school we go away;
Saviour, come, Thy grace revealing,
 In our hearts assert Thy sway;
  Bless us, parting,
On this sacred Sabbath day.

3. Soon our Sabbaths will be ended,
 All our Sabbath hours be past;
Like the leaf to earth descended,
 Withered in the autumn blast;
  Life is passing,—
We must see the grave at last.

OPENING AND CLOSING SCHOOL.

4. Then may heaven be beaming o'er us
   With its glories, sunny bright;
And, with millions saved before us,
   May we join in worlds of light
         Praising Jesus,
Where the Sabbath knows no night.

## 338.

7s.  T. 11.

For a season called to part,
   Let us now ourselves commend
To the gracious eye and heart
   Of our ever present Friend.

2. Jesus, hear our humble prayer:
   Tender Shepherd of Thy sheep,
Let Thy mercy and Thy care
   All our souls in safety keep.

3. What we each have now been taught,
   Let our memories retain;
May we, if we live, be brought
   Often thus to meet again.

4. Then, if Thou instruction bless,
   Songs of praises shall be given;
We'll our thankfulness express,
   Here on earth, and there in heaven.

## 339.

T. 90.

On what in weakness has been sown,
Thy blessing, gracious Lord, bestow;
The power is Thine, yea Thine alone,
To make it spring and fruitful grow:
Do Thou the plenteous harvest raise,
And Thou alone shalt have the praise.

J. Newton.

OPENING AND CLOSING SCHOOL.

S. M.   **340.**   T. 595.

Once more, before we part,
  Bless the Redeemer's name;
Let every tongue and every heart
  Praise and adore the same.

2. Let us upon His word
  Still live, and feed, and grow;
Let us go on to know the Lord,
  And practice what we know.

Hart.

L. M.   **341.**   T. 22.

Dismiss us with Thy blessing, Lord,
Help us to feed upon Thy word:
All that has been amiss forgive,
And let Thy truth within us live.

2. Though we are guilty, Thou art good;
Sprinkle our works with Jesus' blood:
Give every fetter'd soul release,
And bid us all depart in peace.

Hart.

8s. 7s. & 4s.   **342.**   T. 585.

Lord, dismiss us with Thy blessing;
Fill our hearts with joy and peace;
Let us each, Thy love possessing,
Triumph in redeeming grace:
    O refresh us, :||:
Traveling through this wilderness.

2. Thanks we give, and adoration,
For Thy gospel's joyful sound;
May the fruits of Thy salvation
In our hearts and lives abound:
    King of glory, :||:
Sway Thy sceptre all around.

Shirley.

## BENEDICTIONS AND DOXOLOGIES.

### 343.*

The grace of our Lord Jesus Christ, and the love of God, and the communion of the Holy Ghost, be with us all, Amen!

L. M.          **344.**          T. 22.

The grace of our Lord Jesus Christ,
The love of God so highly prized,
The Holy Ghost's communion be
With all of us most sensibly.

                             J. de Watteville.

8s. & 7s.         **345.**          T. 167.

May the grace of Christ our Saviour,
And the Father's boundless love,
With the Holy Spirit's favor,
Rest upon us from above:
Thus may we abide in union
With each other in the Lord:
And possess, in sweet communion,
Joys which earth cannot afford.

                                Newton.

### 346.          T. 185.

The Lord bless and keep thee in His favor
    As His chosen property;
The Lord make His face shine on thee ever,
    And be gracious unto thee;
The Lord lift His countenance most gracious
    Upon thee, and be to thee propitious,
And His peace on thee bestow;
    Amen, Amen, be it so.

                                Latrobe.

\* Appendix, p. 21.

## 347.

8s. & 7s.    T. 167.

Peace be to this congregation,
Peace to every soul therein;
Peace which flows from Christ's salvation,
Peace, the seal of cancell'd sin;
Peace that speaks its heavenly Giver,
Peace, to earthly minds unknown;
Peace divine that lasts for ever,
Here erect its glorious throne.

## 348.

T. 551 or 83.

Now with angels round the throne,
Cherubim and seraphim,
And the church which still is one,
Let us swell the solemn hymn:
Glory to the great I am!
Glory to the slaughter'd Lamb!

2. Blessing, honor, glory, might,
And dominion infinite,
To the Father of our Lord,
To the Spirit and the Word;
As it was all worlds before,
Is, and shall be evermore.

Conder.

## 349.

11s.    T. 39.

To God our Immanuel, made flesh as we are,
Our Friend, our Redeemer, and Brother most dear,
Be honor and glory: Let with one accord
All people say, Amen! Give praise to the Lord.

Gregor.

## 350.

L. M.    T. 22.

Praise God, from whom all blessings flow;
Praise Him, all creatures here below;
Praise Him above, ye heavenly host;
Praise Father, Son, and Holy Ghost.    Bishop Kenn.

## 351.

L. M.     T. 22.

To God the Father, God the Son,
And God the Spirit, Three in One,
Be honor, praise and glory given
By all on earth and all in heaven.

## 352.

C. M.     T. 14.

To Father, Son, and Holy Ghost,
One God, whom we adore,
Be glory, as it was, is now,
And shall be evermore.

## 353.

7s.     T. 11.

Praise the name of God most high,
Praise Him, all below the sky;
Praise Him, O ye heavenly host—
Father, Son, and Holy Ghost!

## 354.

8s & 7s.     T. 18.

Now the Triune God confessing,
God the Father's name adore;
To the Son give praise and blessing:
Bless the Spirit evermore.

## 355.

8s. 7s. & 4s.     T. 586.

Great Jehovah! we adore Thee,
God the Father, God the Son,
God the Spirit, joined in glory
On the same eternal throne:
   Endless praises :||:
To Jehovah, three in one.

## 356.

S. M.                                                                         T. 595.

Ye angels round the throne,
  And men that dwell below,
Worship the Father, love the Son,
  And bless the Spirit too.

*Watts.*

## 357.

S. M.                                                                         T. 595.

To God the Father's throne
Perpetual honors raise;
Glory to God, the eternal Son;
To God, the Spirit, praise.

## 358.

8s & 7s.                                                        T. 167.

Praise the God of all creation,
  Praise the Father's boundless love;
Praise the Lamb, our expiation;
  Praise the Spirit from above:
Praise the fountain of salvation,
  Him by whom our spirits live;
Undivided adoration
  To the One Jehovah give.

## 359.

7s & 6s.                                                       T. 151.

To Thee be praise for ever,
  Thou glorious King of kings;
Thy wondrous love and favor
  Each ransomed spirit sings:
We'll celebrate Thy glory,
  With all Thy saints above,
And shout the joyful story
  Of Thy redeeming love.

ADDITIONAL HYMNS.

## 360.
T. 159.

Sing Hallelujah, praise the Lord,
Sing with a cheerful voice;
Exalt our God with one accord,
And in His name rejoice;
Ne'er cease to sing, Thou ransom'd host,
Praise Father, Son, and Holy Ghost,
Until in realms of endless light
Your praises shall unite.

2. There we to all eternity
Shall join the angelic lays,
And sing in perfect harmony
To God our Saviour's praise;
He hath redeem'd us by His blood,
And made us kings and priests to God;
For us, for us the Lamb was slain:
Praise ye the Lord:—AMEN.

J. Swertner.

---

**ADDITIONAL HYMNS.**

8s. & 7s.
## 361.
T. 167.

Hark, the voice of Jesus crying,
  Who will go and work to-day?
Fields are white, and harvests waiting,
  Who will bear the sheaves away?
Loud and long the Master calleth,
  Rich reward he offers free:
Who will answer, gladly saying,
  "Here am I, send me, send me?"

2. If you cannot cross the ocean,
  And the heathen lands explore,
You can find the heathen nearer,
  You can help them at your door;

If you cannot give your thousands,
  You can give the widow's mite;
And the least you give for Jesus
  Will be precious in His sight.

3. If you cannot speak like angels,
  If you cannot preach like Paul,
You can tell the love of Jesus,
  You can say He died for all.
If you cannot rouse the wicked
  With the judgment's dread alarms,
You can lead the little children
  To the Saviour's waiting arms.

4. Let none hear you idly saying,
  "There is nothing I can do,"
While the sons of men are dying,
  And your Master calls for you.
Take the task He gives you gladly,
  Let His work your pleasure be,
Answer quickly, when He calleth:
  "Here am I, send me, send me."

D. March.

## 362.

10s.*

Abide with me! Fast falls the eventide;
The darkness deepens; Lord, with me abide!
When other helpers fail, and comforts flee,
Help of the helpless, oh, abide with me!

2. Swift to its close ebbs out life's little day;
Earth's joys grow dim, its glories pass away;
Change and decay in all around I see;
O Thou who changest not, abide with me!

3. I need Thy presence every passing hour;
What but Thy grace can foil the tempter's power?
Who like Thyself my guide and stay can be?
Through cloud and sunshine, oh, abide with me!

\* Songs of Gladness, p. 64. [English].

4. I fear no foe with Thee at hand to bless;
Ills have no weight, and tears no bitterness;
Where is death's sting? where, grave, thy victory?
I triumph still, if Thou abide with me!

5. Hold then Thy cross before my closing eyes;
Shine through the gloom, and point me to the skies;
Heaven's morning breaks, and earth's vain shadows flee,
In life, in death, O Lord, abide with me!

H. F. Lyte.

7s. & 6s.* **363.** T. 151.

Jerusalem the golden,
  With milk and honey blest,
Beneath Thy contemplation
  Sink heart and voice oppressed.
I know not, oh, I know not
  What joys await me there,
What radiancy of glory,
  What bliss beyond compare!

2. They stand, those halls of Zion,
  All jubilant with song,
And bright with many an angel
  And all the martyr throng.
There is the throne of David,
  And there from toil released,
The shout of them that triumph,
  The song of them that feast.

3. And they who, with their Leader,
  Have conquered in the fight,
For ever and for ever
  Are clad in robes of white.
Oh land that seest no sorrow,
  Oh state that fear'st no strife,
Oh royal land of flowers,
  Oh realm and home of life!

\* Echo to Happy Voices, No. 126.

ADDITIONAL HYMNS.

4. Oh sweet and blessed country,
　　The home of God's elect;
Oh sweet and blessed country,
　　That eager hearts expect!
Jesus, in mercy bring us
　　To that dear land of rest,
Who art, with God the Father
　　And Spirit ever blest.　Amen.
　　　　　　　　　　Bernard of Cluny.

## 364.

?. M.*

Shall we gather at the river,
　　Where bright angel feet have trod;
With its crystal tide forever,
　　Flowing by the throne of God?
　　　　　CHORUS.
Yes, we'll gather at the river,
The beautiful, the beautiful river,
Gather with the saints at the river
That flows by the throne of God.

2. On the margin of the river,
　　Washing up its silver spray,
We will walk and worship ever,
　　All the happy golden day.
　　　　　CHORUS.

3. Ere we reach the shining river,
　　Lay we every burden down;
Grace our spirits will deliver,
　　And provide a robe and crown.
　　　　　CHORUS.

4. At the smiling of the river,
　　Mirror of the Saviour's face,
Saints whom death will never sever,
　　Lift their songs of saving grace.
　　　　　CHORUS.

* Happy Voices, No. 220.

ADDITIONAL HYMNS.

5. Soon we'll reach the silver river,
   Soon our pilgrimage will cease;
   Soon our happy hearts will quiver
   With the melody of peace.
   CHORUS.

C. M. **365.** T. 14.

Jesus, the very thought of Thee
   With sweetness fills the breast;
But sweeter far Thy face to see,
   And in Thy presence rest.

2. Nor voice can sing, nor heart can frame,
   Nor can the memory find
A sweeter sound than Thy blest Name,
   O Saviour of mankind!

3. O Hope of every contrite heart!
   O Joy of all the meek!
To those who fall, how kind Thou art!
   How good to those who seek!

4. But what to those who find? Ah! this
   Nor tongue nor pen can show;
The love of Jesus, what it is,
   None but His loved ones know.

5. Jesus, our only Joy be Thou,
   As Thou our Prize wilt be;
Jesus, be Thou our Glory now,
   And through eternity!

*Bernard of Clairvaux.*

# INDEX.

## A.

| | Page. |
|---|---|
| Abide with me! | 267 |
| According to Thy gracious word, | 174 |
| A charge to keep I have, | 157 |
| A dread and solemn hour, | 198 |
| Again another fleeting year, | 237 |
| Alas! and did my Saviour bleed, | 74 |
| All glory to the sov'reign Good, | 41 |
| All hail the power of Jesus' name, | 64 |
| All praise to Thee, my God, this night, | 244 |
| All the world give praises due, | 52 |
| Am I a soldier of the cross? | 155 |
| And am I born to die? | 190 |
| And now another hour is past, | 259 |
| And will the Judge descend? | 50 |
| Angels from the realms of glory, | 54 |
| Angels, where'er we go, attend, | 43 |
| Approach, my soul, the mercy seat, | 100 |
| Around the throne of God in heaven, | 211 |
| As birds their infant brood protect, | 169 |
| Assembled in our school once more, | 258 |
| Awake and sing the song, | 138 |
| Awake, my soul, and with the sun, | 238 |
| Awake, my soul, in joyful lays, | 137 |

## B.

| | Page. |
|---|---|
| Begone, unbelief! for my Saviour is near, | 164 |
| Behold a stranger at the door! | 91 |
| Behold the throne of grace, | 148 |
| Beneath our feet and o'er our head, | 186 |
| Be present at our table, Lord! | 247 |
| Be present with Thy servants, Lord! | 249 |
| Be with me, Lord, where'er I go, | 242 |
| Blessed Saviour! Thou hast told us, | 256 |
| Blest are they, supremely blest, | 133 |
| Blest is the tie that binds, | 131 |
| Blest is the work, my God and King, | 176 |
| Blow ye the trumpet, blow, | 222 |
| Bright and joyful is the morn, | 57 |

## C.

| | |
|---|---|
| Children, do you love each other? | 132 |
| Children, hear the melting story, | 94 |
| Children of God lack nothing, | 39 |
| Children of Jerusalem, | 140 |
| Children of the heavenly King, | 141 |
| Christians dismiss your fears, | 79 |
| Christ, my rock, my sure defence, | 196 |
| Christ the Lord, the Lord most glorious, | 53 |
| Come, Holy Spirit, heavenly Dove! | 87 |
| Come, Holy Spirit, on us breathe, | 86 |
| Come, let us join our cheerful songs, | 137 |
| Come, let us join our friends above, | 171 |
| Come, let us join with one accord, | 178 |
| Come, let us sing of Jesus, | 142 |
| Come, Lord, and warm each languid heart, | 203 |
| Come, my soul, thy suit prepare, | 148 |
| Come, Thou Almighty King! | 145 |
| Come, ye sinners, poor and needy, | 89 |
| Come, ye who love the Lord, | 144 |

## INDEX.

### D.

| | Page. |
|---|---|
| Day by day the manna fell, | 42 |
| Day of judgment, day of wonders, | 199 |
| Days and weeks and months returning, | 232 |
| Dearest Jesus, come to me, | 122 |
| Dearest of names, our Lord, our King, | 194 |
| Death has been here and borne away, | 193 |
| Dismiss us with Thy blessing, Lord, | 261 |

### E.

| | |
|---|---|
| Ere mountains reared their forms sublime, | 182 |
| Except the Lord our labors bless, | 255 |

### F.

| | |
|---|---|
| Faith is a precious grace, | 102 |
| Father, whate'er of earthly bliss, | 167 |
| For a season called to part, | 260 |
| For ever here my rest shall be, | 109 |
| For ever with the Lord! | 207 |
| Fountain of wisdom, source of truth, | 251 |
| From all that dwell below the skies, | 84 |
| From Greenland's icy mountains, | 221 |

### G.

| | |
|---|---|
| Gentle Jesus, meek and mild, | 216 |
| Give to our God immortal praise, | 37 |
| Glorious things of Thee are spoken, | 169 |
| Glory to the Father give, | 145 |
| God moves in a mysterious way, | 41 |
| God of every land and nation, | 234 |
| Go, my soul, go every day, | 78 |
| Go to dark Gethsemane, | 73 |
| Go when the morning shineth, | 150 |
| Grant, most gracious Lamb of God, | 115 |
| Great God of nations, now to Thee, | 235 |
| Great God, our feeble efforts own, | 252 |

18

|  | Page. |
|---|---|
| Great God, Thy watchful care we bless, | 235 |
| Great God, we sing that mighty hand, | 238 |
| Great High-priest, we view Thee stooping, | 72 |
| Great Jehovah! we adore Thee, | 264 |
| Guide me, O Thou great Jehovah! | 162 |

## H.

| | |
|---|---|
| Hail, all hail, victorious Lord and Saviour, | 79 |
| Hail Alpha and Omega, hail! | 104 |
| Hail, Church of Christ, bought with His blood, | 156 |
| Hail, Thou once despised Jesus! | 76 |
| Hail, Thou wondrous infant stranger! | 54 |
| Hail to the Lord's anointed, | 62 |
| Happiness, delightful name, | 135 |
| Happy soul, thy days are ended, | 193 |
| Happy the children who are gone, | 212 |
| Hark, my soul! it is the Lord, | 124 |
| Hark the angels singing, | 59 |
| Hark the glad sound! the Saviour comes, | 47 |
| Hark, the herald angels sing, | 55 |
| Hark, the voice of Jesus crying, | 266 |
| Hark, what mean those holy voices, | 57 |
| Hasten, Lord, the glorious time, | 223 |
| Hear the royal proclamation, | 226 |
| Here, gracious God, low at Thy feet, | 252 |
| High in the heavens, eternal God, | 39 |
| Holy Trinity! | 88 |
| Hosanna! raise the pealing hymn, | 71 |
| Hosanna to the living Lord, | 48 |
| How great the bliss to be a sheep of Jesus, | 134 |
| How lost was my condition, | 107 |
| How precious is the book divine, | 34 |
| How serious is the charge, | 255 |
| How shall I meet my Saviour, | 47 |
| How sweet, how heavenly is the sight, | 130 |
| How sweet the name of Jesus sounds, | 109 |
| How sweet Thy dwellings, Lord, how fair, | 180 |

## I.

|  | Page |
|---|---|
| I am a little child, you see, | 214 |
| If Christ is mine then all is mine, | 134 |
| If Jesus Christ was sent, | 99 |
| I hear the words of love, | 108 |
| I know that my Redeemer lives, | 80 |
| I lay my sins on Jesus, | 113 |
| I'll glory in nothing but only in Jesus, | 122 |
| I love the Lord! He lent an ear, | 124 |
| I love the Lord who died for me, | 129 |
| I love Thy kingdom, Lord, | 170 |
| I'm a pilgrim and I'm a stranger, | 202 |
| I'm but a traveler here, | 210 |
| Immanuel, to Thee we sing, | 52 |
| I'm not ashamed to own my Lord, | 154 |
| In duties and in sufferings too, | 67 |
| In mercy, Lord, this grace bestow, | 250 |
| Is God my strong salvation, | 159 |
| I sing th' almighty power of God, | 38 |
| I think when I read that sweet story of old, | 219 |
| I want to be an angel, | 213 |
| I want to be like Jesus, | 70 |
| I was a wandering sheep, | 128 |
| I will a little pilgrim be, | 215 |
| I will rejoice in God my Saviour, | 46 |
| I would not live alway; I ask not to stay, | 191 |

## J.

| Jerusalem, my happy home, | 202 |
|---|---|
| Jerusalem, the golden, | 268 |
| Jesus! and shall it ever be, | 153 |
| Jesus, hail! enthroned in glory, | 82 |
| Jesus, hear our prayer, | 246 |
| Jesus, I love Thy charming name, | 126 |
| Jesus, I my cross have taken, | 152 |
| Jesus, lover of my soul, | 161 |
| Jesus makes my heart rejoice, | 125 |

# INDEX.

|  | Page. |
|---|---|
| Jesus' mercies never fail, | 246 |
| Jesus, my all, to heaven is gone, | 111 |
| Jesus shall reign where'er the sun, | 84 |
| Jesus, tender Saviour, | 216 |
| Jesus, tender Shepherd, hear me, | 220 |
| Jesus, the very thought of Thee, | 270 |
| Jesus, Thou art the sinners' friend, | 101 |
| Jesus, Thy love exceeds by far, | 120 |
| Jesus, where'er Thy people meet, | 180 |
| Jesus, who died, is now, | 81 |
| Joyfully, joyfully onward I move, | 206 |
| Joy to the world! the Lord is come, | 62 |
| Just as I am, without one plea, | 105 |
| Just as Thou art, without one trace, | 93 |

## L.

|  | |
|---|---|
| Laden with guilt and full of fears, | 36 |
| Lamb of God, I look to Thee, | 69 |
| Little children, love each other, | 131 |
| Little drops of water, | 218 |
| Little travelers Zionward, | 187 |
| Lo, He cometh! countless trumpets, | 49 |
| Lo, on a narrow neck of land, | 97 |
| Lord, at Thy table I behold, | 175 |
| Lord, dismiss us with Thy blessing, | 261 |
| Lord, fix our wandering thoughts, | 258 |
| Lord, I am Thine, entirely Thine, | 118 |
| Lord Jesus, we bless Thee that Thou wast a child, | 215 |
| Lord Jesus, who before Thy passion, | 173 |
| Lord of Life, now sweetly slumber, | 78 |
| Lord of the worlds above, | 179 |
| Lord, take my heart just as it is, | 114 |
| Lord, Thou hast called Thy servant home, | 192 |
| Love is the theme of saints above, | 130 |

## M.

| | Page. |
|---|---|
| May Jesus Christ, the spotless Lamb, | 67 |
| May Jesus' grace and blessing, | 241 |
| May the grace of Christ our Saviour, | 262 |
| Mourn for the thousands slain, | 249 |
| My country, 'tis of thee, | 233 |
| My days are gliding swiftly by, | 153 |
| My dear Redeemer, and my Lord, | 66 |
| My faith looks up to Thee, | 110 |
| My faith shall triumph o'er the grave, | 196 |
| My Father, when I come to Thee, | 151 |
| My God, accept my heart this day, | 118 |
| My God a man, a man indeed, | 64 |
| My God, I love Thee! not because, | 127 |
| My God, the covenant of Thy love, | 119 |
| My God, the spring of all my joys, | 135 |
| My Saviour God, my sov'reign Prince, | 172 |
| My soul, awake and render, | 240 |
| My soul, be on thy guard, | 157 |
| My times are in Thy hand! | 168 |

## N.

| | |
|---|---|
| Nearer, my God, to Thee, | 162 |
| Not all the blood of beasts, | 167 |
| Not what these hands have done, | 112 |
| Now be the Gospel banner, | 225 |
| Now is past the time of teaching, | 259 |
| Now I lay me down to sleep, | 246 |
| Now let our hearts rejoin, | 243 |
| Now the shades of night are gone, | 242 |
| Now the Triune God confessing, | 264 |
| Now to the Lord a noble song! | 139 |
| Now with angels round the throne, | 263 |

## O.

| | |
|---|---|
| O Comforter, God, Holy Ghost, | 85 |
| O could we but love that Saviour, | 123 |

## INDEX.

|  | Page. |
|---|---|
| O'er the realms of pagan darkness, | 228 |
| O Father of mercy, be ever ador'd, | 88 |
| O for a thousand tongues to sing, | 44 |
| O happy day that stays my choice, | 115 |
| O head so full of bruises! | 77 |
| O how soft that bed must be, | 167 |
| O Lord, forgive a sinful child, | 100 |
| O Lord, how vile am I, | 95 |
| O love, thou fathomless abyss, | 103 |
| O mother dear, Jerusalem, | 204 |
| Once more before we part, | 261 |
| One prayer I have,—all prayers in one, | 165 |
| One sweetly solemn thought, | 183 |
| One there is above all others, | 119 |
| On Jordan's banks the baptist's cry, | 49 |
| On Jordan's stormy banks I stand, | 205 |
| On what in weakness has been sown, | 260 |
| O send forth the Bible, more precious than gold, | 226 |
| O Son of God and man receive, | 66 |
| O Spirit of the living God! | 87 |
| O tell me no more, | 154 |
| O the delights, the heavenly joys, | 83 |
| O 'tis a folly and a crime, | 185 |
| O timely happy, timely wise, | 241 |
| Our heavenly Father, source of love, | 89 |
| Over the ocean wave, far, far away, | 227 |
| O where shall rest be found, | 98 |

### P.

| | |
|---|---|
| Palms of glory, raiment bright, | 209 |
| Peace be to this congregation, | 263 |
| Plunged in a gulf of dark despair, | 44 |
| Poor and needy though I be, | 166 |
| Praise God, from whom all blessings flow, | 263 |
| Praises, thanks and adoration, | 147 |
| Praise the God of all creation, | 265 |
| Praise the name of God most high, | 264 |

INDEX.

| | Page. |
|---|---|
| Praise to Thee, O Lord, we render, | 146 |
| Prayer is the soul's sincere desire, | 147 |
| Precious Saviour, of salvation, | 229 |
| Present your bodies to the Lord, | 114 |
| Preserved by Thine almighty power, | 230 |

## Q.

| | |
|---|---|
| Quiet, Lord, my froward heart, | 40 |

## R.

| | |
|---|---|
| Remember thy Creator now, | 185 |
| Rise, my soul, and stretch thy wings, | 184 |
| Rock of ages, cleft for me, | 105 |

## S.

| | |
|---|---|
| Saviour, breathe an evening blessing, | 243 |
| Saviour—King! in hallowed union, | 250 |
| Saviour, like a shepherd lead us, | 218 |
| Saviour of Thy chosen race, | 96 |
| See, my soul, God ever blest, | 65 |
| See the kind shepherd, Jesus, stands, | 92 |
| Shall we gather at the river, | 269 |
| Show pity Lord, O Lord forgive, | 96 |
| Sing Hallelujah, praise the Lord, | 266 |
| Sinners turn, why will ye die? | 91 |
| Softly the night is sleeping, | 60 |
| Songs of praise the angels sang, | 143 |
| Sovereign of worlds! display Thy power, | 225 |
| Sow in the morn thy seed, | 253 |
| Stand up, my soul, shake off thy fears, | 158 |
| Stand up, stand up for Jesus! | 158 |
| Sun of my soul, Thou Saviour dear, | 243 |
| Sweeter sounds than music knows, | 56 |
| Sweet the moments, rich in blessing, | 75 |

## T.

|  | Page. |
|---|---|
| Teacher divine, we bow the knee, | 254 |
| Teach me, my God and King, | 67 |
| Teach me the measure of my days, | 190 |
| Thanks and praise, :‖: | 33 |
| The author of salvation, | 63 |
| The Bible, the Bible more precious than gold, | 35 |
| Thee we address in humble prayer, | 246 |
| Thee we adore, eternal name! | 181 |
| Thee will I love, my strength and tower, | 121 |
| The grace of our Lord Jesus Christ, | 262 |
| The hour of sleep is now at hand, | 245 |
| The hours' decline and setting sun, | 244 |
| The lambs of Jesus, who are they, | 132 |
| The Lord ascendeth up on high, | 80 |
| The Lord bless and keep thee in His favor, | 262 |
| The moment comes, the only one, | 189 |
| The Saviour's blood and righteousness, | 106 |
| The Sunday-school army has gathered once more, | 231 |
| The voice of free grace cries: escape to the mountain, | 45 |
| The wise men from the East adored, | 61 |
| There is a fountain fill'd with blood, | 75 |
| There is a happy land, far, far away, | 261 |
| There is a house not made with hands, | 200 |
| There is a land of pure delight, | 200 |
| There is a time, we know not when, | 183 |
| There's a song the angels sing, | 58 |
| This day belongs to God alone, | 177 |
| This is the day the Lord hath made, | 178 |
| Thou dear Redeemer, dying Lamb, | 126 |
| Thou holy, spotless Lamb of God, | 46 |
| Thou, Jesus, art our King, | 136 |
| Though but a little child I am, | 214 |
| Thy law is perfect, Lord of light, | 34 |
| Time, what an empty vapor 'tis, | 181 |
| To Father, Son, and Holy Ghost, | 264 |
| To God, our Immanuel, made flesh as we are, | 263 |

## INDEX.

| | Page. |
|---|---|
| To God the Father, God the Son, | 264 |
| To God the Father's throne, | 265 |
| To God, the only wise, | 139 |
| To the hills I lift mine eyes, | 160 |
| To Thee be praise for ever, | 265 |
| To Thee, God Holy Ghost, we pray, | 86 |
| To Thee, O blessed Saviour, | 229 |
| 'Twas by an order from the Lord, | 33 |
| 'Twas the commission of our Lord, | 173 |

### U.

| | |
|---|---|
| Unveil thy bosom, faithful tomb, | 197 |

### W.

| | |
|---|---|
| Watchman, tell us of the night, | 223 |
| We are but young, yet we may sing, | 220 |
| We are not orphans on the earth, | 166 |
| We are out on an ocean sailing, | 188 |
| We bring no glittering treasures, | 232 |
| We come to sing Thy praise, | 257 |
| We sing Thy praise, exalted Lamb, | 83 |
| We speak of the realms of the blest, | 208 |
| Welcome, delightful morn, | 177 |
| Welcome, sweet day of rest, | 176 |
| We're traveling home, to heaven above, | 93 |
| What a mercy, what a treasure, | 36 |
| What good news the angels bring, | 51 |
| What praise to Thee, my Saviour, | 247 |
| What secret hand at morning light, | 239 |
| What shall I render to my God, | 116 |
| What various hindrances we meet, | 149 |
| When for some little insult given, | 69 |
| When gathering clouds around I view, | 163 |
| When I can read my title clear, | 106 |
| When I survey the wondrous cross, | 74 |
| When Jesus into Salem rode, | 72 |

|  | Page. |
|---|---|
| When little Samuel woke, | 217 |
| When rising from the bed of death, | 198 |
| When shall the voice of singing, | 224 |
| When we devote our youth to God, | 117 |
| Where high the heavenly temple stands, | 81 |
| Where two or three with sweet accord, | 256 |
| While, with ceaseless course, the sun, | 236 |
| Whither, pilgrims, are you going? | 205 |
| Who are these in bright array? | 209 |
| Who shall sing, if not the children? | 143 |
| Why should we start and fear to die, | 238 |
| With humble prayer, oh, may I read, | 37 |
| Witness, ye men and angels now, | 116 |

## Y.

| Ye angels round the throne, | 265 |
|---|---|
| Ye servants of God, your great Master proclaim, | 141 |

# TUNES.

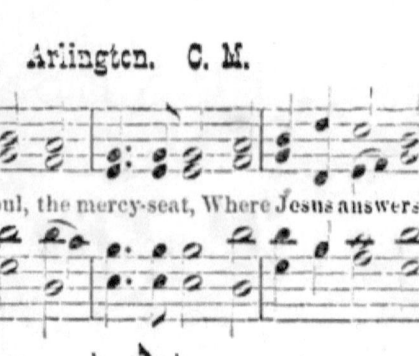
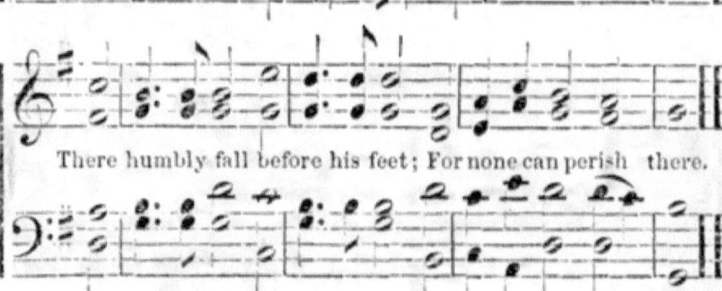
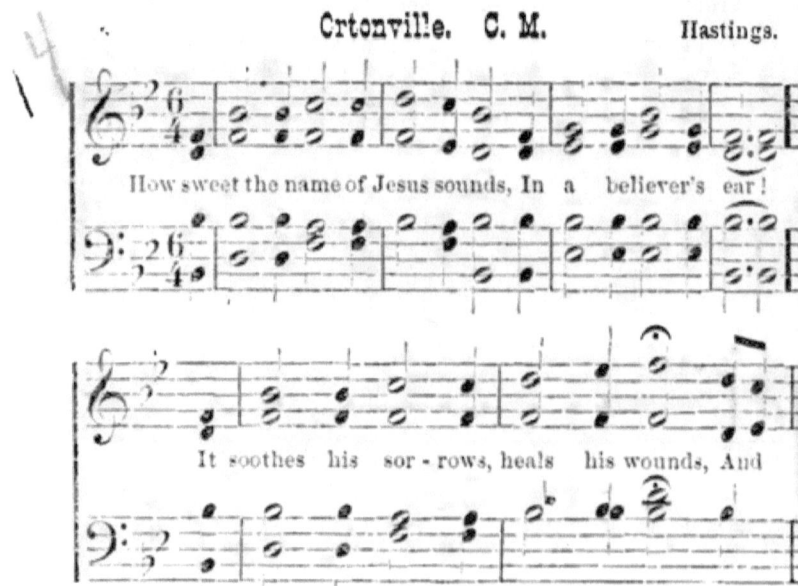

Sa-viour and my God! Well may this glow-ing heart re-joice, And tell thy good-ness all a-broad.

## ZADOC. 7s. 6 lines.

1. Rock of Ages, cleft for me! Let me hide myself in thee.
D.C. Be of sin the double cure, Cleanse me from its guilt and pow'r.

Let the water and the blood From thy riven side that flowed

Of nations in commotion, Prepared for Zion's war.

### Portuguese Hymn. 11s.

How firm a foundation, ye saints of the Lord, Is laid for your faith in his excellent word! What more can he say than to you he hath said, You who unto Jesus for refuge have

2 Jesus, our Lord, arise,
  Scatter our enemies;
    Now make them fall!
  Let thine almighty aid
  Our sure defence be made,
  Our souls on thee be stay'd:
    Lord, hear our call!

3 Come, thou incarnate Word,
  Gird on thy mighty sword;
    Our prayer attend!
  Come, and thy people bless;
  Come, give thy word success;
  Spirit of holiness,
    On us descend!

## Saviour, like a Shepherd lead us. 8s, 7s, & 4s. 15

Saviour, like a shepherd lead us, Much we need thy tend'rest care;
We are thine, do thou befriend us, Be the Guardian of our way;

In thy pleasant pastures feed us, For our use thy folds prepare.
Keep thy flock, from sin defend us, Seek us when we go astray.

Blessed Jesus, Blessed Jesus, Thou hast bought us, thine we are;
Hear young children when they pray,

Blessed Jesus, Blessed Jesus, Thou hast bought us, thine we are.
Hear young children when they pray.

## The Morning Star.

F. F. Hagen.

Morning star! thy cheer-ing light Can dis-pel the gloom of night; Light divine, come and shine, Come and shine, Light di-vine, In this dark-some heart of mine.

Thine effulgence, glorious light,
Far exceeds the sun so bright;
Jesus, thou canst bestow,
Jesus, thou canst bestow
More than thousand suns can do.

Joyful beam, thy light we see,
Willingly we follow thee;

Fairest Star, near and far,
Near and far, Fairest Star,
Christ as God, we thee revere.

Therefore, oh, thou Light divine,
Come without delay and shine;
Jesus come, make thy home,
Jesus come, make thy home
In my heart; Lord Jesus, come.

### Single Chants. No. 1.

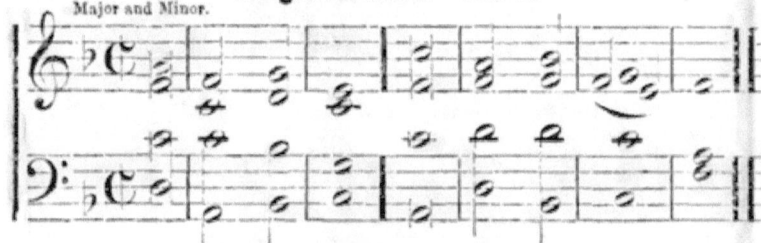

### No. 2.  Dr. Aylward, c. 1784.

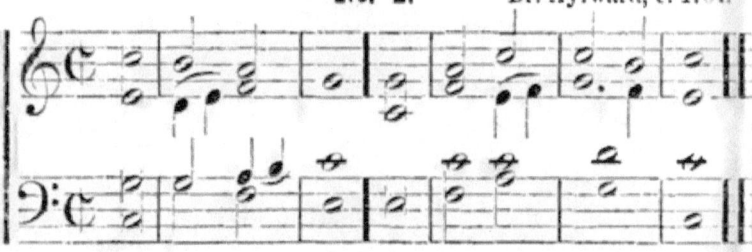

### No. 3.  W. L. Viner, c. 1824.

www.ingramcontent.com/pod-product-compliance
Lightning Source LLC
Chambersburg PA
CBHW022110230426
43672CB00008B/1332